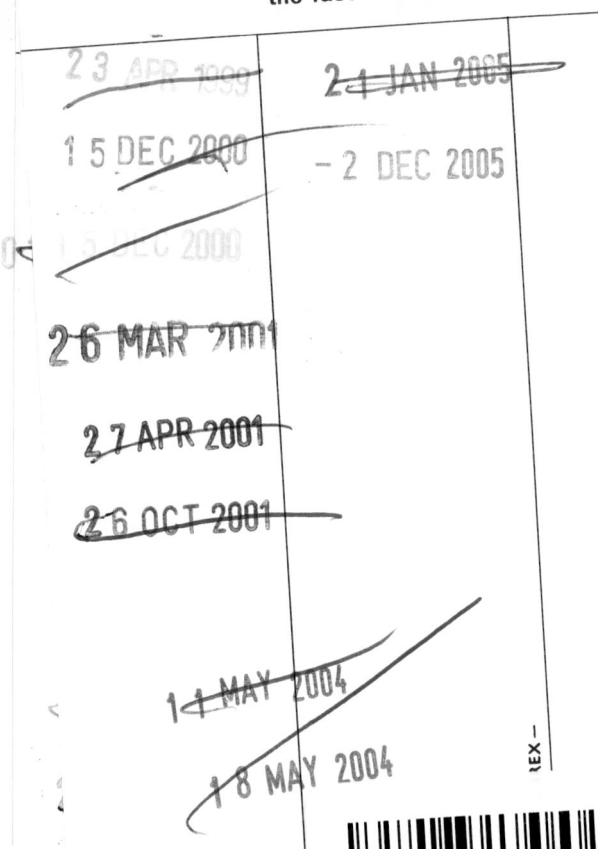

JAPANESE ECONOMIC DEVELOPMENT

JAPANESE ECONOMIC DEVELOPMENT

A Short Introduction

YOSHIHARA KUNIO

TOKYO
OXFORD UNIVERSITY PRESS
OXFORD NEW YORK MELBOURNE

Oxford University Press
OXFORD LONDON GLASGOW
NEW YORK TORONTO MELBOURNE WELLINGTON
KUALA LUMPUR SINGAPORE HONG KONG TOKYO
DELHI BOMBAY CALCUTTA MADRAS KARACHI
NAIROBI DAR ES SALAAM CAPE TOWN

First published 1979
Reprinted 1981

ISBN 0 19 580439 2

Printed in Singapore by Dainippon Tien Wah Printing (Pte) Ltd.
Published by Oxford University Press, 3, Jalan 13/3,
Petaling Jaya, Selangor, Malaysia

To the memory of
Mr. and Mrs. Nakamura Shigeichi

Preface

In the past fifteen years or so, a considerable amount of interest in Japanese economic development has been generated outside Japan. Those concerned with international relations desire to understand the process and nature of Japanese development in order to evaluate better the dimensions of Japan's economic impact on international relations. Knowledge of Japanese economic development has also served as useful background information for those looking for an opportunity to penetrate the Japanese market; for those seeking ways to protect domestic industry in the face of mounting imports from Japan; and finally, for those aiming to attract greater amounts of Japanese aid and investment.

There is another dimension to the growth of interest in Japanese economic development. That it was an essentially capitalistic development that took place in a traditional (at least, non-revolutionary) setting, had important political implications in the Cold War environment of the post-war period. The United States, increasingly concerned with the spread of communism in Asia after Mao's victory in the Chinese Civil War, began looking for a non-revolutionary model of development and supported the rise of interest in Japanese economic development as part of the ideological campaign.

In spite of associations with the Cold War strategy of the United States, there was no denying that Japanese economic development was an interesting intellectual challenge to observers of social change. For example, that capitalistic development occurred in a non-Western setting destroyed many stereotypical notions about economic development. The Protestant ethic which, according to Max Weber, played an important role in capitalistic development in the West, did not have any relevance in Japan since Japanese culture was largely unaffected by Christianity. Nor had democracy been a precondition for Japanese economic development; in fact, there were remnants of feudalism in the modern period. The Japanese experience also demolished the racist notion that the developed areas of the world were restricted to those inhabited by Caucasians, as the American geographer, E. Huntington (*Civilization and Climate*, New Haven, Yale University Press, 1924), had asserted in the pre-war period.

Japan's rapid growth in the post-war period, sometimes called an economic miracle, became a target of envy of the developing countries; at the same time, it raised their hopes for rapid development. By learning the 'secrets' of such rapid growth, they hoped to follow the same course. Their initial hopes were dashed to some extent when it became clear later on that in Japan's case there had been a lengthy period of preparation for growth: yet Japanese development continued to interest those who wanted to draw practical lessons relevant to the post-war setting.

There are already a number of books written on Japanese economic development, and the necessity for yet another may be questioned. Several times in the past decade, I have been asked to teach courses in Japanese economic development at foreign universities. Each time, I have had difficulty in choosing textbooks and even basic references for students. Since most of the students were undergraduates, I could not assume any deep interest on their part in Japanese economic development. To satisfy their needs, it would have been best to use a short book as the basic reading, but such a one did not exist.

One alternative would have been to compile basic readings from articles and chapters in various books, but I often ended up discussing subjects not covered by the reading, or by giving a different emphasis and interpretation, for I have a somewhat different perspective from most English speaking writers on Japanese economic development. For example, writings by Japanese Marxists are largely ignored in the major English works on Japanese development. I do not agree with most of the Marxist interpretations and analyses, but they do have certain valid points and throw new light on certain aspects of the Japanese development process, so they cannot be simply brushed aside as totally irrelevant.

Another reason why my approach is somewhat different is that I deal with Japanese development within a general framework of economic development. I am not interested in peculiarly Japanese problems; instead, I focus on what I consider to be major development issues from my experience in South and South-East Asia. From this perspective, it became necessary to change the priority of topics in discussion to include non-economic factors of development. How the task which seems so difficult for countries in South and South-East Asia was overcome in Japan is one of the points emphasized in this book.

Since there is a vast amount of literature on Japanese economic development, it is almost impossible to survey it all. Whenever my writings are related to publications in English, the sources are indicated. Japanese sources are cited, but not very extensively, for I assume that the reader would not, in any case, be able to read them.

The organization of this book is as follows. Chapter I gives an overall view of the development process in the past century. Chapter II puts Japanese economic development in a comparative framework, and discusses what are considered to be its distinguishing features. Chapter III deals with trade and development: more specifically, how trade patterns have changed over time, what accounts for these changes, and to what degree trade has stimulated Japanese development. The fourth chapter, going back to the mid-nineteenth century, takes a close look at the initial conditions of development, and contrasts Japan's preparedness for development with that of other Asian countries. Chapter V discusses institutional reforms in the early Meiji era and post World War II occupation, which had a large impact on Japanese economic development. The last chapter deals with pathological aspects of Japanese development, and re-examines the desirability of taking Japanese development as a model for development.

The present work, which covers the past century, would clearly have been impossible without the past writings of Japanese scholars, to whom my first acknowledgement goes. On a personal level, various people helped me gain new insight into Japanese economic development. I would like to thank Dale Jorgenson for helping me develop theoretical tools to analyse the problems of economic development when I was a graduate student, Ichimura Shin'ichi and Yasuba Yasukichi for discussing various problems relating to the Japanese economy, Ron McKinnon for clarifying some ambiguities on the relationship between trade and development during my stay at Stanford, and Sakata Yoshio for elucidating the basic historical trends around the time of the Meiji Restoration. Finally, I would like to express my appreciation to Bernard Gordon, Lorraine Harrington, Thomas Huber, Carl Mosk and Alan Woodhull, who commented on the first draft of the manuscript. Needless to say, any faults or mistakes in the final version are my sole responsibility.

Otsu, Japan
August 1978

YOSHIHARA KUNIO

Contents

Tables

Figures

Author's Notes

IN this work, Japanese names appear in the normal Japanese order: surname first and given name second.

For the reader's convenience, specialized terms relating to Japanese history are collected in the Glossary, and major historical events (since the early 1850s) in the Chronological Table. Both appear at the end of the volume.

1955~73

I

The Course of Economic Growth

ECONOMIC development, which transformed Japan into a modern country, is sometimes regarded as a post World War II phenomenon, but its beginning goes back many years. In this chapter, discussion on the Japanese development process begins with 1868, the year when an important political change known as the Meiji Restoration[1] took place and a new government determined to carry out modern measures was born. To start with 1868 does not mean, however, that Japan suddenly emerged out of a primitive state in that year. Prior to 1868, there was social and political development, and a degree of economic progress. Since it was after the Meiji Restoration, however, that machine production and other qualitative changes in the economic life of Japan began, it is justifiable to take the year 1868 as the great watershed.

1868–1885

In the first seventeen years of the Meiji era, Japan broke out of the fetters of feudalism and made the transition into a new economic age. In the first several years, social and political reforms were carried out to do away with various feudal institutions of the Tokugawa period (1603–1867). First, the decentralized Tokugawa political system was abolished to bring about political integration of the country, and then, feudal restrictions and privileges were revoked for the establishment of a new society based on merit and individual initiative.[2] It was also necessary to modernize monetary and fiscal systems, and to educate people in the necessity of adopting modern Western technology. Since these tasks took another several years, it was not until the mid-1880s that a new economic system was firmly established and the economy was set on a path of long-run growth.

The Tokugawa fiscal system was too cumbersome for a modern state: the rice tax (which accounted for the bulk of government revenue in the period) was paid in kind; tax rates varied by province, and were subject to the conditions of harvest. In order to create a monetary tax whose rate was uniform throughout the country, the Meiji government instituted a tax reform which led to the establishment of a new land tax. Besides being a uniform monetary tax (as required of a modern form of taxation), the land tax was also important in that it accounted for the bulk of the tax revenue in the first few decades of the Meiji era and was the major financial source of government expenditure for developmental purposes. Furthermore, by making the taxpayer of the land its legal owner, the land tax conferred alienability on the land and laid the foundation for the private property system.

The Tokugawa monetary system was also an obstruction to the economic integration which the Meiji government wished to achieve. Under the late Tokugawa system, there was no central control over the issue of money. Paper money was issued by local governments, and coins were minted by the shogunate. There were, as well, some regional differences in the money standard. In Osaka, prices were expressed in terms of the weight of silver, whereas in Edo,[3] merchants used different units[4] to express the price of commodities, and these depended primarily on gold coins. Furthermore, the difference in the relative prices of gold to silver between Japan and the West caused a large outflow of gold from Japan after trade with the West began.[5]

In 1871, a monetary reform was carried out to establish

a standardized and sound currency for the country. For this purpose, the authority to issue money was made the monopoly of the central government. The cumbersome Tokugawa monetary standard was replaced by the decimal system with the yen as the basic monetary unit, and money carrying the new denomination was issued for use throughout the country.[6] Furthermore, the gold standard was adopted, and paper notes issued on a convertible basis.

The last task was, however, difficult. First, the gold standard was already collapsing in the mid-1870s. The government designated the gold coin as the standard, but also minted one yen silver coins to be circulated in restricted areas in order to facilitate transactions among merchants engaged in foreign trade. The silver coin had the same metallic content as the Mexican dollar (which was widely accepted as a means of payment among foreign traders in Asia), and was made equivalent to the one yen gold coin at the ratio of sixteen units of silver to one unit of gold. Because of a large discovery of silver in the United States, and a few other factors, however, the price of silver began to decline in 1875, and the price ratio of silver to gold became twenty to one in the following year. Since the conversion rate remained the same in Japan, silver coins were brought into the country to exchange for gold coins, and there was a renewed outflow of gold from Japan. To make up for the scarcity of gold coins, the government had to approve the unrestricted use of silver coins, and thus adopted, *de facto*, the silver standard.

The convertibility of paper notes became difficult for internal reasons. In the first several years of the Meiji era, because political instability limited the ability of the government to collect taxes, expenditures exceeded revenues by a large margin. In fact, the bulk of expenditure was met by issuing paper notes. This accelerated around the mid-1870s when the government wished to increase military expenditure in order to suppress rebellions by opponents of modernization measures. To make the situation worse, because the government allowed national banks to use government bonds[7] as the reserve for their notes, the issuing of paper notes further escalated towards the end of the 1870s. As a consequence, paper notes circulated at discount values.

In 1881, Matsukata Masayoshi became Minister of Finance, and began to withdraw paper notes from circulation by creating surpluses in the government budget, causing the so-called 'Matsukata deflation'.[8] He reduced government expenditure, created new taxes and redeemed paper notes with the surpluses thus created. He continued this policy until his retirement in 1885 when the convertibility of notes was virtually restored. During his tenure as Minister of Finance, the Bank of Japan was established as the only bank of note issue, and the basis for a conservative monetary management was laid.[9]

One major economic activity of the Meiji government in this period was the building of the country's infrastructure. In 1869, the government decided to construct railroads, and in 1872, the first line was completed between Tokyo and Yokohama. In subsequent years, railroad mileage increased fairly rapidly: from 18 miles in 1872 to 212 miles in 1885, to 580 miles in 1889 when the Tokaido line from Tokyo to Kobe was completed. Sea transportation was also modernized by importing steamships from the West. The government did not operate shipping lines directly, but gave large subsidies to Iwasaki Yataro to build a fleet of modern merchant vessels to handle the increasing volume of sea transportation.[10] The government also modernized the network of communications by introducing postal and telegraphic services. At the end of this period, there were over 5,000 post offices handling about 100 million pieces of mail per year. Major telegraph lines in the country had been completed and the number of private messages handled per year approached 3 million. In addition, overseas telegraph communications became possible when Nagasaki (in the island of Kyushu) was linked to the undersea cable from Shanghai which was, in turn, connected all the way to London and New York. In contrast, however, to the rapid development of the telegraph system, there was little progress in extending telephone service in this period.

Since the scale of modern enterprises required capital beyond what one merchant or one family could command, the joint-stock company (which pools capital from different people) was promoted as the form of enterprise most suitable for the new period. In 1871, for the first time, joint-stock companies were formed in the fields of transportation, finance and land reclamation. In manufacturing, the first joint-stock company was established in 1873 for silk-reeling.[11] It was around this time that men like Shibusawa Eiichi and Godai Tomoatsu resigned their government posts in order to enter into business as private individuals, and to persuade tradition-bound merchants of the merits of the new forms of enterprise. Consequently, from the mid-1870s on, more and more people became convinced of the value of joint-stock companies. By 1885, there were 1,279 companies with capital amounting to 50 million yen.

A new, dynamic economy necessitated the wide use of machines in industrial production, and the government took various measures to lead the economy in this direction. By importing machinery from the West and inviting foreign technicians, the government-operated mines and factories in textiles, metals, cement, glass and shipbuilding.[12] Government production itself did not amount to much, but provided a model to open the eyes of investors as to what methods of production could be like in the new period. Spinning, which the government envisioned as the first industry to undergo an industrial revolution, was given first priority. Spindles were leased out on favourable terms and low interest loans were given to those wishing to establish spinning mills. In the period 1880–2, the government used 350,000 yen for this purpose, and an additional 100,000 yen was spent for experiments in spindle production. Furthermore, a number of delegations were dispatched to industrial exhibitions abroad to allow them the opportunity of observing industrial progress in the West.

Despite these government initiated measures, no great progress was achieved during this period in spreading the use of machines. Even in spinning, the highest priority industry, machine-spun yarn was still only a small part of total yarn consumption, accounting (in 1882–4) for only about 6 per cent of total consumption and 25 per cent of domestic production. Domestic yarn, which was therefore mostly hand-spun, barely survived under the pressure of import competition from the West; yet, with about 60,000 modern spindles installed by the end of 1885, machine production gradually gained in importance. In paper, steel and shipbuilding as well, the proportion of machine production rose. Although in general, the significance of machine production in terms of absolute amounts was small, its rise in these industries signalled the beginning of the machine age in Japan.

1886–1911

In the remaining twenty-five years of the Meiji era, a 'miracle' was achieved. This small, backward country called Japan, which had hardly attracted any attention, astonished the world by winning two major wars and thus earned the right to join the ranks of Great Powers. Such an unexpected increase in Japan's power can rightly be called a 'miracle'. When economic miracles are spoken of in the context of Japan, the successes of the post World War II period come quickest to mind; actually, this was the second miracle Japan accomplished—the first one was worked during the Meiji era.

The military strength of Japan was first demonstrated by its victory in the Sino-Japanese War (1894–5), in which Taiwan was obtained as a colony. Then, in 1905, Japan defeated Russia in a war fought over the question of Korea and China. The fact that it was a victory over a Western country raised Japan's prestige in the world considerably. After this, Japan was accepted for the first time as a full-fledged nation by the Western Powers, and the last inequality in the treaties signed in 1858 (the 5 per cent ceiling on the tariff rate Japan could impose on imported goods) was removed. But this was not enough, for Japan now wanted to establish supremacy over all East Asia, and in 1910 Korea fell prey to this expansionist policy.

Behind the Meiji miracle was solid economic development. As in the 1870s, the government played an active role in building up the infrastructure of the country. In 1885–1911, the mileage of government-operated railroads increased from 212 miles to 4,775 miles; the number of post offices increased from about 5,000 to 7,000, and the amount of mail handled per year from about 100 million to 1,500 million pieces; the number of telegraph offices increased from about 50 to 4,500, and the number of telegrams handled per year from about 3 million to 25 million. In addition, the availability of telephone service began to spread after 1892, and by 1911 about 180,000 households and offices had telephones. Under government encouragement, private capital also contributed to this infrastructure building. In 1911, there were about 1,400 miles of private railroad line and about 1,800 privately owned steamships, which amounted to 1,375,000 tons. Also, electric power supply began to increase in the early 1900s, and in 1911 Japan possessed a 322,000 kwh capacity.

The most remarkable aspect of the economic development in this period was the rise of the cotton textile industry. In the mid-1880s, yarn spun by machine was still a small part of total consumption. Soon after, however, large-scale spinning mills were established, and hand-spinning gradually disappeared. The next task was to eliminate imports, but this took another ten years or so. In 1891, Japan began to export to China, and then in 1897, for the first time, exports exceeded imports. By the end of this period, spinning was firmly established as an export industry. In addition, the establishment of a Japanese spinning mill in Shanghai in 1911 foreshadowed the growing importance of overseas investment.

Import substitution of cotton fabric was delayed until 1909. Probably because of the rudimentary state of the power-loom, the hand-operated loom remained important until relatively late. In order to compete with imported fabric, however, it was necessary to switch to machine production, and this was first undertaken by spinners who were also engaged in weaving. By the 1890s, some had even begun to export to China. The rapid increase of machine production had to wait until around 1905 when the increase of wages as a result of the past growth and the availability of electric power began to make it more attractive for small-scale hand-weavers to switch to power-looms. After this, both production and exports increased at a rapid pace, and imports declined sharply.

One of the most characteristic features of the textile industry was its resilience. The opening of trade with the West in the mid-nineteenth century caused havoc with the traditional Japanese textile industry, but it did not succumb to the import challenge. By adopting the new technology, it gradually recovered its share in the domestic market and finally succeeded in phasing out imports, without the aid of trade protection. This fact alone is noteworthy but, more remarkably, the textile industry established itself as an export industry soon after import substitution was completed.

Mechanization and technological progress also took place in other industries. In the sugar industry, several modern refineries were set up after Taiwan became Japan's colony and the government took measures to increase its sugar-cane production. In shipbuilding, in 1898, Japan built a steel ship of about 6,000 tons which qualified, for the first time, for Lloyd's insurance, which was known for the strictness of its standards. Then, in 1908, two steel ships which measured 13,000 tons each were built. By 1910, Japan had developed a capacity to build most military ships and more than half of the civilian steamships newly ordered.[13] Mechanized silk-reeling became increasingly prevalent and around the mid-1890s, factory production exceeded household production. In iron and steel, in 1901, a large-scale steel mill (Yahata Steel) began operation, and the amount of pig iron production (which had been hovering around 20,000 tons per year before the opening of the mill) increased to about 200,000 tons several years later. By 1910, domestic production accounted for about half of pig iron consumption and about one-third of steel consumption.

The increased use of machines in industrial production in this period is reflected in the following trends. The number of factories utilizing steam or electric power increased from 53 to 7,745. The increase was partly due to the appearance of private power companies. Also, the imports of industrial machinery from the West increased. In the previous period, the import value of industrial machinery had been about 300,000 yen per annum on the average, but in this period it increased to 12 million yen. Furthermore, the amount of paid up capital in industrial companies reached the 500 million yen mark by the end of the period—fifty times the amount at the beginning of the period. It would be reasonable to assume that a large part of this increase was used to finance the purchase of machinery.

In agriculture, changes took place within a traditional setting, and were not as revolutionary as in industry. Nonetheless, development was quite impressive, as can be seen from the index of agricultural production which increased at an annual rate of about 2 per cent in this period. This increase was of course slower than in industry, but it was a significant break from the stagnation of the Tokugawa period.[14] The production of rice (then the major agricultural product) increased by about 30 per cent over this period. Particularly important among the various factors accounting for this increase was the introduction of new strains of rice responsive to fertilizer application and resistant to cold. As the economic activities of farm households diversified, raw silk also emerged as an important product. Over the period, the number of farm households engaged in silk production increased and the total production rose about six times. Towards the end of this period, silk became, next to rice, the most important product.

Since agriculture was still the most important sector of the economy, its growth affected the overall performance, and in this respect, what happened in agriculture was significant. Furthermore, as industrial production increased, more and more people moved from agricultural production to consumption. Consequently, an increasingly large percentage of the population was forced to purchase food. If this requirement had not been met by domestic production, subsequent food importation would have caused a drain on foreign exchange and constrained industrialization. Agricultural production increased rapidly enough in this period, however, to meet the food requirement. Also, the land tax revenue was an important contribution to the government budget, and made it possible to allocate funds for the promotion of industry. Furthermore, increased production of tea and raw silk (the latter in particular) made it possible to earn the foreign exchange necessary to buy machinery and industrial raw materials from abroad. In short, agriculture played an important supportive role in Japanese industrialization; without the vigour of agriculture, the rapid pace of industrialization in this period would have been inconceivable.[15]

1912–1936

Agriculture continued to play a supportive role in industrialization, but its significance was much diminished in this period. First, the industrial sector became less dependent on Japanese agriculture for food supply. Since the

Japanese government promoted agricultural development while discouraging industrial production in the colonies (Taiwan and Korea) acquired in the previous period, a pattern emerged in the trade between Japan and its colonies in which Japan exported industrial goods and imported agricultural products. In 1925, imports from the colonies accounted for 18 per cent of rice, 67 per cent of wheat, 126 per cent of soy bean, and 44 per cent of adzuki bean production in Japan.[16] Agriculture also declined in importance as an earner of foreign exchange. The exports of raw silk increased until the end of the 1920s and continued to be the major foreign exchange earner, but cotton fabric emerged in this period as another important foreign exchange earner. Raw silk finally lost its position as the major foreign exchange earner in the early 1930s when the demand for raw silk declined due to the economic depression in the United States. Furthermore, the financial contribution from agriculture to industry decreased, despite the increased tax burden per farm household, as agricultural income became an increasingly smaller percentage of national income. By the late 1920s, it was exceeded by industrial income, and in 1936 it became less than 20 per cent of the total.[17]

In exports, the rise of light industrial goods was impressive. First, there was the rapid increase of cotton fabric production. During this period Japan dethroned Manchester from its position as the world centre of textile production. This may be called the most glorious age in the history of the cotton textile industry in Japan. Silk fabric also became an important export commodity as part of the raw silk produced began to be woven and exported in the form of fabric. In the 1930s, the exports of garments and rayon fabric expanded rapidly—more than compensating for the decline in silk exports. By the mid-1930s, the products of light industry began to dominate Japanese exports. Supported by the increase in export demand, yarn production increased 3.2 times, cotton fabric 6.2 times, silk fabric

8.6 times, and light industry as a whole 3.6 times.

From the above, it might be inferred that light industry became the dominant sector of industry, but on the contrary, there was a significant decline in its importance relative to heavy industry. In the beginning of this period, light industry employed 85 per cent of factory workers, but at the end, the percentage had declined to 60. In terms of production, the percentage declined from 80 to 50. Thus, despite a remarkable performance in exports, light industry ceded its predominant position to heavy industry.

The beginning of heavy industry can be traced back to the end of the Tokugawa period, when the shogunate and provincial governments introduced Western technology to produce modern weapons. From that time, industrialization signified, at least in part, development of the armaments industry and was promoted primarily for military purposes.[18] In the early phase of industrialization, the government directly operated factories for the production of iron and steel, weapons, shipbuilding and precision machinery; but, from the mid-1880s, by relying on subsidies, protection from foreign competition and other indirect measures, the government encouraged the private sector to enter into heavy industry. The only major exception to the policy of non-direct participation was the establishment of Yahata Steel. In other words, heavy industry did not suddenly appear in this period, but in the earlier periods it had been much less noticeable, and its foundation was weak. In this period, due to the overall economic progress and the accelerated military build-up in the 1930s, there was rapid industrialization of this sector. By the end of the period, there had emerged a fairly well developed industrial complex in Japan.

In the development of heavy industry, it is important to note the impact of World War I. Japan was a participant in the war on the side of the Allies, but since there was no prospect of serious fighting in Asia, there was no need for military build-up. Thus, the impact of the war on heavy industry was not from the military, as in the 1930s; it was rather an economic impact. The war brought about unprecedented prosperity within the Japanese economy, and this was generally conducive to investment in heavy industry. In addition, the halt of imports of machinery, parts and intermediate goods from the West brought about a sharp increase in their prices and created a favourable economic environment for their production in Japan.

The war boom did not, however, last long. The war ended in late 1918, and a few years later the West returned to recapture former markets in Japan. Nevertheless, it had to face the high tariff barriers erected by the government to protect the import substitution industry created during the war. This was, in fact, the first time Japan used the tariff autonomy it had regained in 1911 to give protection to domestic industry.

One characteristic of this period was that the economy was subject to serious cyclical disturbances. The years 1914–19 were the most prosperous for the Japanese economy. World War I reduced the economic capacity of the West and brought about an overall shortage of goods. Due to past progress, Japan was in a good position to take advantage of the situation. During the period 1914–18, a surplus of 1,475 million yen was recorded in the trade account, and from 1915 to 1920, a 2,207 million yen surplus was recorded in the invisible account. Because of such huge surpluses, the supply of money increased sharply, and consequently, prices increased 2.7 times from 1915 to 1920. In this inflationary setting, since cost increase lagged behind price increase, the rate of profits increased in general, and companies recording over 100 per cent profit rates were not exceptional. Stimulated by such increased profitability, a large number of new companies were formed, and most existing ones expanded production capacity. As a result, the amount of industrial capital increased from 644 million yen to 2,829 million yen between 1913 and 1920.

The boom continued for about eighteen months after the war ended, but in the spring of 1920, the first reaction set in. In contrast with the American economy, which enjoyed prosperity in the 1920s, the Japanese economy experienced a gloomy decade. The economy suffered not in the sense that indicators of the real sector of the economy were at a lower level in the 1920s than in earlier years, but in the sense that many companies suffered losses, bankruptcies were numerous, and large numbers of people were in debt or unemployed. In 1923, a great earthquake occurred in the Tokyo area and further set back the economy which had begun to show signs of recovery. In 1927, there was a financial crisis which shook people's confidence in banks. Then, in 1929, the crash of the American stock market led the way to the depression in the West of the 1930s. The resulting decline in the American market adversely affected Japan's exports of raw silk and silk fabric. The economic downturn continued until 1932 when the government took expansionary measures, and prices, which had been declining since 1920, began to increase.

The progress of heavy industry and the recession of the 1920s brought about an increase in economic concentration. The trend toward concentration is most notable in the area of finance. The number of banks (which had been increasing up to 1901) declined after that point, reflecting the government policy of encouraging mergers. Until the end of World War I, however, the rate of the decline was slow; it was not until the 1920s that there was a significant increase in concentration. In this decade, because of numerous bankruptcies, banks ended up with bad debts, and those which were mismanaged began to face serious difficulties. These difficulties culminated in the financial crisis of 1927 when approximately thirty banks, including a few large ones, closed their doors and the government declared a moratorium on debts. The disappearance of small or badly managed banks continued in the following years, and by the end of the period, a small number of large banks, such as Mitsui, Mitsubishi, Sumitomo and Yasuda had established dominant positions.[19]

In heavy industry, output concentration is more or less expected since the relatively high level of technology and the large amount of capital necessary for entry act as barriers. Shipbuilding, iron and steel, and general machinery, which had shown some progress in earlier periods, were oligopolies dominated by a few giant companies. At that time, however, output concentration did not attract much attention since light industry was relatively more important and characterized by the presence of large numbers of small companies. Spinning was somewhat exceptional since there were large companies occupying an important position in that industry. Even in this case, barriers to entry were not as high as in a typical heavy industry, as reflected in the existence of a large number of small spinning companies. As heavy industry progressed, the competitive structure of light industry receded into the background, and the oligopolistic structure of heavy industry established itself as the typical structure of industry as a whole.

Increase in output concentration is an important development in this period, but it is not a characteristic unique to the Japanese economy; it may be observed in any capitalistic country. What became alarming in Japan, however, was that several *zaibatsu* (family controlled commercial combines) began to exert important influences on the economy in the latter part of the period. Among them, Mitsubishi, Mitsui and Sumitomo were the most diversified and powerful. Through holding companies they controlled companies in finance, mining, industry and other modern sectors of the economy. These *zaibatsu* did not appear suddenly; some even pre-dated the Meiji era, and even before World War I, they operated banks, mining companies and other enterprises. Yet, it was not until after the war that they became particularly noticeable. In the 1920s they vigorously moved into heavy industry, took over companies which were suffering from heavy losses, and used holding companies to extend control over a greater number of companies through partial ownership. The government, far from taking measures to reduce the economic power of the *zaibatsu*, prompted their growth by means of subsidies, tariff protection, approval of cartel formation and other measures designed to encourage expansion of *zaibatsu* activity in heavy industry. In the 1930s when the government desired further expansion in heavy industry for military purposes, the relation between the government and the *zaibatsu* became particularly close, and the latter evolved into powerful politico-economic organizations.

1937–1951

This period covers what may be termed the 'abnormal' years of modern Japanese economic history. The first phase of the period comprised the war years, beginning with the outbreak of war against China in June 1937 and continuing for eight years until the end of the Pacific War. The second phase, the Occupation years, began with Japan's surrender on 15 August 1945, and lasted until April of 1952 when sovereignty was restored. The last year of this period, 1951, is the last full year of the occupation.

The year 1937 marked an important turning point in Japanese economic development. First, the financial orthodoxy established by Matsukata in the mid-1880s, which had been instrumental in maintaining price stability in the following years, was abandoned. Although government expenditures had been increasing since 1931, the increase was still moderate prior to 1936 because people like Takahashi Korekiyo (a financial conservative) objected to sharp increases in military expenditures through bond issue.[20] By the end of 1936, however, most influential conservatives had either been assassinated or forced to change their views, the military held sway, and government expenditures began to increase rapidly. From 1936 to 1937, government spending more than doubled, and in the following three years, it doubled again.

The second major event of 1937 was the passage of laws empowering the government to impose direct controls on the economy. Soon after the war broke out, three important decisions were made. The Armament Mobilization Law (which had been passed during World War I) was made applicable to the present war, and the government was given authorization to take mobilization measures to step up armament production. The Law Relating to Temporary Measures for Export and Import Control was enacted to give the government absolute power over exports and imports, and the Temporary Adjustments Law to funnel capital and credit to war-related industries and stop the flow to non-essential industries was also passed.

Not satisfied with these measures alone, the military pressured the government to enact the National Mobilization Law in April 1938. This gave the government power to control prices and wages and to institute distribution control. Thus, within several months after the war broke out, all legal measures necessary to move to a mobilization economy were completed.

One might argue that to take 1937 as a turning point is too arbitrary since government control actually began early in the 1930s. In 1931, the Major Industries Control Law was passed, and the formation of cartels in important industries was encouraged to facilitate government control. In 1933, the Exchange Control Law was passed to restrict non-essential imports. These laws certainly increased the scope of government intervention, but they were not designed to abolish the price system and to run the economy by command. For example, in the top priority iron and steel industry, in keeping with the spirit of the Major Industries Control Law, a new company called Japan Steel Manufacturing was formed by merging Yahata Steel and several private enterprises. It controlled 90 per cent of pig iron production, but its control of steel was only 50 per cent. The companies which decided to opt out retained a considerable degree of autonomy in steel production. After the outbreak of the war in 1937, government control of production and consumption became applicable to all companies, but it was not until late 1941 when the Iron and Steel Control Association was set up that the government exercised really stringent control over the industry. (This association was also set up in line with the Major Industries Association Ordinance issued in accordance with the mobilization power of the government.)

Because of the havoc caused to the economy by the Pacific War, it would be natural to think that income had declined during the war. It was not until the last year of the war, however, that real GNP declined, and in fact, there was a 25 per cent increase over the period 1940–4. This does not mean that there was an increase in the general economic welfare over those years, for the main component of the increase was military expenditure (which increased by about 430 per cent over the same period). Consumption, on the other hand, decreased by 30 per cent. Furthermore, the increase in real GNP was maintained by scrapping non-military hardware and mobilizing those who did not work under normal circumstances. It seems, therefore, that in terms of all conceivable indexes, there was a substantial decline in welfare over the period.

Changes in the industrial structure during the war are noteworthy. Production in light industry, which consisted primarily of non-essential goods, declined absolutely as well as relatively. The two laws passed to restrict production of non-essential goods after the war broke out in 1937 were, for the most part, responsible for the beginning of the decline. For example, cotton textile production, which had recorded remarkable growth by the end of the previous period, declined sharply after September 1937 when the Law Relating to Temporary Measures for Export and Import Control allowed importation of raw cotton only for export; production declined still further after the importation of cotton became difficult due to the outbreak of the Pacific War. In 1944, the level of textile production stood at about 90 per cent below the peak of mid-1937. On the other hand, production of heavy industry rose prior to mid-1944 due to the government policy of concentrating available resources on steel, non-ferrous metals and machinery essential to the war effort. Because such priorities existed, the share of heavy industry in total industrial production continued to rise from 50 per cent in 1936 to more than 70 per cent in 1942.

There was another important development which occurred as government control on the economy tightened. In order to establish more effective economic control and obtain greater efficiency in the utilization of scarce resources, the government preferred to deal with only a small number of large companies in each industry and pressed for mergers by using mobilization measures as a weapon. This policy further increased the economic power of the *zaibatsu*. They were in a good position to take advantage of government policy, not only because their companies were large and could take initiatives in merger, but also because they could use the political power they had acquired to influence the government committees or industry associations which were in charge of the actual mergers. By the end of the war, in terms of paid up capital, the share of the four largest *zaibatsu* had increased to 50 per cent in finance, 32 per cent in heavy industry and 11 per cent in light industry; the share of the ten largest amounted to 53 per cent in finance, 49 per cent in heavy industry and 17 in light industry.[21]

Although total output increased from 1943 to 1944, procurement of raw materials for the production of steel and non-ferrous metals became increasingly difficult. As a result, production declined slightly from 1943 to 1944, despite various efforts to bolster it. The overall increase from 1943 to mid-1944 was made possible by utilizing available stocks and increasing production of machinery and other final goods.

By mid-1944, Japan had lost naval supremacy and had been cut off from its overseas territories, a major source of raw materials. As a result, production of basic materials began to decline sharply, affecting, in turn, the production of final goods. By the beginning of 1945, the economy had developed acute shortages of oil, bauxite, iron ores, and other essential raw materials. Then, the intensified bombing attacks in the last several months of the war delivered the final blow to the already tottering economy.[22]

At the time Japan surrendered, the economy was to a large extent shattered. In August 1945, industrial production was down to a small percentage of what it had been a year earlier, and amounted to only about 10 per cent of the 1934–6 level. Food production, which had been maintained at a relatively high level despite the shortage of manpower and fertilizer, declined by about 30 per cent in 1945. As a consequence, a food crisis developed towards the end of the year which continued until the first half of 1946. The shortage of goods was made more acute by the breakdown of the government machinery for the collection and distribution of goods at fixed prices. The defeat caused a loss in confidence in the government, and brought about a condition of near anarchy.

Economic recovery had to be undertaken under difficult conditions. Bombing by the Allies had destroyed about 25 per cent of the national wealth.[23] Among other things, it had caused an acute shortage of housing in the major cities. The loss of colonies meant not only that natural resources could no longer be obtained at concessionary rates, but also that several million Japanese in the colonies had to return to look for jobs and houses in the already crowded home market. Japanese overseas assets, which had provided income as well as a basis for overseas operations in the pre-war period, were confiscated. In addition, the demands of the occupation forces for such services as housing and transportation had to be met. Furthermore, changes in the political environment in the Asian countries which had been important markets for Japanese exports before the war dimmed hopes of using the pre-war industrial strategy for economic recovery.

The chaotic condition of the post-war economy is reflected in the hyperinflation which occurred from mid-1945 to early 1949. For a few months before the surrender, the tempo of price increases quickened and became somewhat alarming, but it was nothing compared with what took place thereafter. The consumer price index (with 1945 as the base) rose to 515 in 1946, 1,655 in 1947, 4,857 in 1948, and 7,889 in 1949—a total increase of approximately 8,000 per cent. Fortunately, despite such economic chaos, production increased. In 1948, industrial production returned to 50 per cent of the 1934–6 level, while food production made a full recovery.

In 1949, the government undertook a new stabilization policy whose top priority was to stop inflation through expenditure cuts and tax increases in the government budget. This anti-inflation measure was reinforced by the adoption in April 1949 of the single exchange rate of 360 yen to $1. It was then necessary for the government to monitor the movement of prices and to adjust monetary policy accordingly in order to maintain the fixed exchange rate. As these measures became effective in securing economic stability, the government removed various measures of direct control. By mid-1950, the market economy had been essentially restored.

The stabilization measures adversely affected companies which were badly managed or overextended, but on the whole, had a favourable effect on the economy. Economic recovery progressed smoothly in 1949 and the first half of 1950. In June 1950, when the Korean Conflict[24] broke out, Japan came to be used as a supply base as well as a place of 'rest and relaxation' for American soldiers. The demand for Japanese goods and services rose sharply, and the economy experienced the first boom of the post-war period. The boom gave a final push to economic recovery, and allowed many companies to reap large profits. A large percentage of these profits was retained in companies and used later for plant renewal and expansion, and for introduction of technology from abroad.

Economic recovery was greatly influenced by the occupation policies. At first, the Allies followed a policy of non-responsibility, as indicated in a directive of November 1945 to the Supreme Commander of the Allied Powers (SCAP) stating that 'You will make it clear to the Japanese people that you assume no obligation to maintain any particular standard of living in Japan'.[25] In 1946, food aid began as a means of forestalling a famine which threatened the country. By this time, the SCAP had assumed, at least, the responsibility of preventing disease and unrest, and by the end of the year, had decided to allow the economy to return to pre-war levels. In line with this policy, aid in the form of oil, iron ores, coal, and other raw materials necessary for Japanese industry was initiated. Finally, by the end of 1948, SCAP was strongly encouraging the Japanese government to take measures to stabilize the economy, and to promote economic development beyond pre-war levels. Thus, within three-and-a-half years, there had been a drastic change in the occupation policy: a shift from an attitude of non-responsibility to the promotion of economic development.

The basic reason for such a change was that the United States, which essentially shaped the occupation policy, had developed a positive view of Japan's role in the security of post-war Asia, for as the Cold War between the United States and Soviet Union intensified, American policy towards Japan became more favourable. In 1948, civil war in China was progressing in favour of the communists, and this seems to have pushed the United States to support Japan fully as the country with the best chance of contributing to the security of Asia by becoming a counterforce to communism.

In line with this new policy, the United States not only pursued a more favourable economic policy in Japan, but also initiated a move to end the occupation. Initially, the United States faced objections from its allies, but finally succeeded in persuading them to come to the conference table. Under its auspices, the San Francisco Peace Conference was held in September 1951, and in April of the following year, the occupation of Japan formally ended. The fact that it was the United States that shaped occupation policy and restored Japan's sovereignty conditioned the domestic and international framework of the Japanese economy in the post-war period.

1952–1973

No overall increase in GNP or per capita income occurred during the previous period, because the war interrupted the growth trend. There were, however, large differences in growth potential between 1937 and 1951. One such difference lay in the social and political environment of the economy. Soon after Japan's unconditional surrender in August 1945, the Allied occupation forces disarmed the country and reorganized the government along democratic lines. To support the new political goals, land reform, labour reform, education reform, and dissolution of the *zaibatsu* were carried out. Consequently the post-war society became more égalitarian and competitive, and because of the commitment to peace, the heavy weight of military expenditure was greatly lightened.

It is essential also to note the change in industrial capability for generating economic growth. During the war years, investment and technical progress took place in many war-related sectors of heavy industry, and by the end of the war, Japan had reached a high level of technological sophistication. The disappearance of military demand and the pent-up demand for consumption goods caused the importance of heavy industry to decline in the immediate post-war period. The experiences and experiments of the war years, however, provided a basis not only for developing new products with great growth potential, but also for absorbing new Western technology; all of which made it possible for heavy industry to spearhead post-war economic growth.

Changes in the international environment also raised the growth potential of the post-war economy. Because Japan now had become an ally of the United States, economic co-operation between the West and Japan increased. Barriers to the transfer of technology to Japan which had existed in the 1930s were now removed, and new Western technology became more readily available. This was important particularly because Japan could now take advantage of the backlog of science-based technology which had developed rapidly during the 1930s and 1940s. The first major application of basic science had been in the field of chemistry, resulting in the production of synthetics and antibiotics. The post-war period witnessed industrial applications of physics, stimulated primarily by United States government spending in missile technology and the space programme. Advances in electronics were also made at this time, and when these new discoveries were made available to Japanese industry, they made an important contribution to technical progress.

Closer economic contacts were also made possible by the Bretton Woods system established in the early post-war years. One pillar of the new system was the General Agreement on Tariff and Trade (GATT) which is based on the notion that free trade is the best means of enhancing a people's well-being. The GATT has not yet achieved the goal of free trade but has been effective in reducing tariff and non-tariff barriers and abolishing discriminatory practices in international trade. The International Monetary Fund (IMF), the second pillar of the new system, contributed to a more stable monetary environment for international trade by championing the fixed exchange rate system and freer international transactions by pressing its member countries to remove foreign exchange restrictions on trade. Under this new system, the economies of different countries became more closely integrated.

For a country like Japan which greatly depends on foreign trade for economic development, this new economic system was particularly valuable. It not only made it possible to increase the volume of trade and enjoy a greater gain from trade, but also contributed to increased efficiency by subjecting Japanese companies to international competition and enlarging the size of the market. It is commonly acknowledged that export-oriented companies had to strive constantly for greater efficiency because of competition in the export market. What is often forgotten, however, is that even those whose markets were mainly domestic had to face foreign competition as imports became liberalized and tariffs were reduced. Under the new economic system, by the early 1970s, the Japanese had become closely integrated with the international economy.

By the end of the occupation, agricultural production, industrial production, national income, per capita income, per capita consumption, labour productivity, real wages and most other indicators of economic development had returned to the 1934–6 level, but there was one exception: trade did not return to the pre-war level until much later.[26] Export, for example, was less than 40 per cent of the pre-war level in 1952, and did not recover fully until 1960. This was due to various difficulties facing exports in the post-war setting. Political changes in Korea, Taiwan and China (countries which had accounted for about 40 per cent of Japan's exports in the pre-war period) reduced their market potentiality in the post-war period. Cotton textiles, the major export in the pre-war period, faced a difficult situation because of the import-substitution policy in those markets. The demand for silk (another important export in the pre-war period) shrank because of the appearance of a substitute, nylon. And the fact that Japan had not yet concluded all necessary commercial treaties handicapped exports, throughout the early 1950s.[27]

A major barrier to the increase of exports was the change in the structure of export demand in favour of heavy industrial goods, and therefore, it became imperative for Japan to develop competitiveness in these international markets. Large subsidies for plant expansion and renewal were given to encourage the introduction of more up-to-date machinery and technology. Construction of large industrial estates along the coast allowed better coordination of industrial production and transportation costs were minimized. Furthermore, the policy of protecting and promoting the domestic coal industry was scrapped, and oil was substituted for coal, or where technically unfeasible, better and cheaper coal was imported.[28]

By 1960, this policy began to pay off. By then, heavy industry had improved its international competitiveness in ships, radios, steel, cement and several other products which had become the propelling force of Japanese exports.[29] By the mid-1960s, passenger cars, synthetic fibres and new electronic products such as tape recorders joined the list of major exports, driving total Japanese exports to a much higher level. Consequently, the volume of export returned in 1960 to the pre-war level, and increased about seven times in the following thirteen-year period. In this process of rapid overall expansion, textile products which had weighed so heavily in the pre-war period became insignificant, whereas the heavy industrial goods, previously unimportant or non-existent, came to dominate.

The export increase made an important contribution to industrial production. Over this period, industrial production increased by about 2.7 times, recording an annual growth rate of about 13 per cent. By virtue of this rapid increase, in 1972, Japan became the world's largest producer of synthetic fibres, rubber, pig iron and passenger cars; and the third largest producer of pulp, nitrogen fertilizer, cement, steel, copper and aluminium. Industrial production not only increased in volume but also diversified to include synthetic rubber, synthetic fibres, petrochemicals, electronic goods and other newly developed products. By the early 1970s, in terms of both volume and diversity, Japanese industry had become one of the most advanced in the world.

Spurred by industrial expansion, other sectors of the economy grew quite rapidly, and as a consequence, the GNP (a measure of the economic activity of all sectors) recorded a large increase. From 1952 to 1958, GNP increased at a rate of 6.9 per cent. Even so, it was not until 1959, when the growth rate exceeded 10 per cent, that any serious world-wide attention was paid to the Japanese economy. In the following year, the growth rate surpassed that of the previous year, and Japanese economic growth was termed an economic miracle.

To the astonishment of all, this high growth rate was maintained through the 1960s. In this decade, the annual increase in GNP averaged 10 per cent. In 1970–3, the growth rate declined slightly to 7.8 per cent, but even this was high by international standards.

As the Japanese economy grew, it increasingly attracted world attention. In 1950, Japanese GNP amounted to $24 billion, smaller than that of any Western country and only several per cent of the American GNP. In the following years, however, Japan's GNP surpassed all Western countries except the United States; it had exceeded that of Canada by 1960, Britain and France by the middle of the decade, and West Germany by 1968. In 1973, Japanese GNP was about $360 billion, and while still smaller than the American GNP, the difference had narrowed to three to one—a considerable gain from 1950. Even though per capita income did not grow as spectacularly during this period as the GNP, there were substantial increases which continue to the present day. In terms of export and economic aid as well, Japan's international standing rose significantly during this period.

The period of rapid growth was brought to a sudden end by the oil crisis which began in October 1973. The first phase of the crisis was an oil embargo imposed by the OPEC nations on industrial countries in order to pressure them into taking a pro-Arab stand on the fourth Middle Eastern War which had commenced a short time earlier. Because the embargo ended shortly, its effect was temporary, but the decision by the OPEC nations to triple oil prices had a more lasting impact. In Japan, where dependence on imported oil for energy is high, GNP showed a negative growth rate in 1974, for the first time in the postwar period. Thereafter, it became positive once again, and the GNP has recorded slight increases since the oil crisis. It is generally thought, however, that the recession is not yet over; the number of unemployed is still large with no sign of decline, and the number of bankruptcies continues at a high level. Especially alarming is the minimal increase in industrial production—a dynamic growth force before the oil crisis, but now, more of a drag on recovery. At the time of this writing, it is not clear when the recession will end. But, when it does, because of the fundamental changes which have occurred in the international environment, it is unlikely that the pattern of growth in the period prior to the oil crisis will be resumed.

1. The Meiji Restoration refers to the political events of 1868 which deposed the Tokugawa regime and returned power to the emperor. His reign (1868–1912) is called the Meiji ('enlightened rule') era.

2. The first section of Chapter V discusses Meiji institutional reforms in more detail.

3. Tokyo was called Edo in the Tokugawa period.

4. These units were called *ryo*, *bu* and *shu*.

5. Foreign trade was virtually prohibited during most of the Tokugawa period.

6. The yen is the unit of Japanese money in the modern period. In the early 1870s, 1 yen was roughly equivalent to US$1. By 1897, the yen had devalued to 2 yen per US dollar. From then until 1931, the exchange rate remained at about the same level (although in the early 1920s, there was a tendency for the yen to devalue). In 1932, the yen devalued sharply, and the rate remained for the rest of the 1930s at approximately 4 yen per US dollar. In the post-war years, the exchange rate was set at 360 yen to the dollar in 1949, and remained at that level until December 1971. The yen then revalued to 308 to the dollar, and this rate was maintained until February 1973. Since then, the trend has been toward the revaluation of the yen. At the time of writing (August 1978), US$1 is worth about 180 yen.

7. In the Tokugawa period, the samurai (the ruling warrior class) received their salaries in rice. The Meiji government took over the financial responsibility to support the former samurai, but instead of continuing the same system, it decided to commute their rice stipends to government bonds bearing interest at rates from 5 to 6 per cent. At first, commutation was voluntary, and then, in 1876, it became compulsory. Government bonds handed to samurai totalled about 190 million yen.

8. The Matsukata deflation is discussed further in the section on price increase in Chapter II.

9. On the question of Matsukata's encounter with Leon Say, a conservative Minister of Finance in France in the late 1870s, and Say's possible influence on Matsukata's financial orthodoxy, see H. Rosovsky, 'Japan's Transition to Modern Economic Growth, 1868–1885' in H. Rosovsky (ed.), *Industrialization in Two Systems: Essays in Honor of Alexander Gerschenkron*, New York, John Wiley and Sons, 1966, p. 133.

10. Iwasaki Yataro was the founder of Mitsubishi, one of the four largest *zaibatsu* in the pre-war period.

11. Tsuchiya Takao and Okazaki Saburo, *Nihon Shihonshugi Hattatsu Shi Gaisetsu* [Historical outline of the development of Japanese capitalism], Tokyo, Yuhikaku, 1937, pp. 117–21.

12. For government involvement in industry in the early Meiji, see T. C. Smith, *Political Change and Industrial Development in Japan: Government Enterprises, 1868–1880*, Stanford, Stanford University Press, 1955.

13. Takahashi Kamekichi, *Meiji Taisho Sangyo Hattatsu Shi* [History of industrial development in the Meiji and Taisho eras], Tokyo, Kaizo Sha, 1922, pp. 520–2.

14. T. C. Smith argues that there was considerable technological

progress in Tokugawa agriculture and challenges the view that it was stagnant. See *The Agrarian Origins of Modern Japan*, Stanford, Stanford University Press, 1959. But even if this view is accepted, it would be reasonable to argue that there was a significant break in the trend of productivity increase.

15. On the role of agriculture in this period, see K. Ohkawa and H. Rosovsky, 'The Role of Agriculture in Modern Japanese Economic Development', *Economic Development and Cultural Change*, October 1960.

16. Takahashi, op. cit., p. 411.

17. K. Ohkawa *et al.*, *National Income: Estimates of Long-Term Economic Statistics of Japan Since 1868*, Vol. 1, Tokyo, Toyo Keizai Shinposha, 1974, Table 9.

18. J. Dower (ed.), *Origins of the Modern Japanese State: Selected Writings of E. H. Norman*, New York, Pantheon Books, 1975, pp. 225–34.

19. Mitsui, Mitsubishi, Sumitomo and Yasuda were the four largest *zaibatsu* (family controlled commercial combines) in the pre-war period.

20. Takahashi Korekiyo (1854–1936) held various cabinet posts including that of Minister of Finance from the mid-1910s to 1936 when he was assassinated.

21. E. Hadley, *Anti-Trust in Japan*, Princeton, Princeton University Press, 1969, Chapter 3.

22. J. Cohen, *Japan's Economy in War and Reconstruction*, Minneapolis, University of Minnesota Press, 1949, pp. 104–9. Also, consult this source for Japan's war preparation in the 1930s and the state of the economy during the war.

23. Economic Planning Agency, *Sengo Keizai Shi: Sokan Hen* [History of the post-war economy: overview], Tokyo, Printing Bureau, Ministry of Finance, 1957, pp. 9–12.

24. Although the Korean Conflict lasted until July 1953, major hostilities ended in July 1951, when truce talks began.

25. Cohen, op. cit., p. 417.

26. Economic Planning Agency, *Keizai Hakusho* [Economic survey of Japan], 1952; hereafter cited as *Keizai Hakusho*.

27. *Keizai Hakusho*, 1953, p. 32.

28. *Keizai Hakusho*, 1960, p. 42.

29. Light industrial goods include food products, textiles, wood products, ceramics and glass products, printing and publishing, and miscellaneous manufactured goods, whereas heavy industrial goods include chemicals, iron and steel, non-ferrous metals, and machinery (including electronic products).

II

Characteristics of Japanese Development

ECONOMIC GROWTH

IF to learn the historical process is the first step to understanding Japanese development, the next step would be to put it in a comparative framework and examine how Japanese development differs from that in other countries. Of course, it is impossible to deal with all differences: even if it could be done, it would not be very meaningful. Thus, when the development of one country is compared with that of another country, emphasis tends to be placed on their basic differences. When Japan is put in comparison with Western countries or developing countries of today, what are its basic characteristics? How did they come into existence? This chapter attempts to answer these questions.

Simon Kuznets defines modern economic growth as a long-run upward trend in income which results in a dramatic change in economic life.[1] Modern economic growth in these terms took place first in Britain in the second half of the eighteenth century, and then spread within the next century to other Western European countries and their overseas offshoots. In view of the similarity of key institutions and values, the fact that the British growth caused a chain reaction among Western countries might not be surprising, but it was more striking that it triggered modern economic growth in Japan, a distant country which does not share a common cultural background with the West.

As shown in Table 1, Japan's modern economic growth started relatively late: it was not until the fourth quarter of the nineteenth century. But once it started, the pace of

TABLE 1

Modern Economic Growth

	Period	*Rates of Growth per Decade (%)*			*Coefficients of Multiplication in a Century*		
		Total Product	*Popula-tion*	*Product per capita*	*Total Product*	*Popula-tion*	*Product per capita*
U.K.	1765/85 to 1963–7	23.7	10.1	12.4	8.4	2.6	3.2
France	1831–40 to 1963–6	21.8	3.2	18.1	7.2	1.4	5.3
Belgium	1900– 4 to 1963–7	20.3	5.3	14.3	6.3	1.7	3.8
Netherlands	1860/70 to 1963–7	27.7	13.4	12.6	11.5	3.5	3.3
Germany	1850– 9 to 1963–7	31.0	10.8	18.3	14.9	2.8	5.4
Switzerland	1910 to 1963–7	26.3	8.8	16.1	10.4	2.3	4.5
Denmark	1865– 9 to 1963–7	32.5	10.2	20.2	16.6	2.6	6.3
Norway	1865– 9 to 1963–7	31.4	8.3	21.3	15.3	2.2	6.9
Sweden	1861– 9 to 1963–7	37.4	6.6	28.9	23.9	1.9	12.6
Italy	1895– 9 to 1963–7	31.4	6.9	22.9	15.3	2.0	7.8
Japan	1874– 9 to 1963–7	48.3	12.1	32.3	51.4	3.1	16.4
U.S.A.	1834–43 to 1963–7	42.4	21.2	17.5	34.4	6.9	5.0
Canada	1870– 4 to 1963–7	41.3	19.0	18.7	31.8	5.7	5.6
Australia	1861– 9 to 1963–7	36.4	23.7	10.2	22.3	8.4	2.7

Source: S. Kuznets, *Economic Growth of Nations*, Cambridge, Harvard University Press, 1971, pp. 4–14.

Note: When years in stubs are connected by a slash (/), data are for the single years indicated; when connected by a dash (–), they are for all years in the interval.

growth was remarkably fast. According to the Table, the rate of growth of total product per decade was 58.3 per cent, the highest among the developed countries and more than twice that of Belgium, Britain, and France. Also in the growth of per capita income, the Japanese performance was remarkable: 32.3 per cent per decade, higher than in any other country.

One unique feature of Japanese growth is that the rate of growth has increased over time, or as Ohkawa and Rosovsky put it, there has been 'a trend acceleration'.[2] At first, the growth rate was relatively modest; it stepped up in 1910 and reached its peak in the post-war period. This should be contrasted with the time pattern of growth in other countries. In the British case, the time pattern is an inverted V-shape: growth peaked in the second half of the nineteenth century and then declined. In the French case, the pattern is the opposite of the British: the growth rate first declined, bottomed out in the early twentieth century, and then rose in the following years. Unlike these two cases, Japanese growth accelerated over time as if growth fed growth.

Japanese modern economic growth began from a subsistence level of income. Western countries, on the other hand, started from a relatively high level of income. As shown in Table 2, per capita income in the West at the beginning of modern economic growth ranged (in 1965 prices) from Britain's $227 to Australia's $930. Even the lowest British level was about three times as high as per capita income in Japan. Japan's figure of $74 is comparable to that of developing countries in Africa and Asia.

What the figure of $74 implies is that there had been practically no increase in per capita income in the period before the beginning of modern economic growth. Output and population had increased without affecting the level of income. Agricultural output increased over time as a result of acreage increase or technological innovation, and this increase contributed to population increase. In turn, popula-

TABLE 2
Approximate Product Per Capita
At the Beginning of Modern Growth
(Developed Countries)

		Extrapolation to Initial Date		
	GNP per capita, 1965 (US$) (1)	*Date*[1] (2)	*Reduction Factor (Growth)* (3)	*GNP per capita, Initial Date, 1965 $ (col. 1/col. 3)* (4)
1. United Kingdom–Great Britain	1,870	1765–85	8.23	227
2. France	2,047	1831–40	8.46	242
3. Belgium	1,835	(1865)	3.80	483
		(1831–40)	5.63	326
4. Netherlands	1,609	(1865)	3.27	492
		(1831–40)	4.64	347
5. Germany[2]	1,939	1850–9	6.41	302
6. Switzerland	2,354	(1865)	4.45	529
7. Denmark	2,238	1865–9	6.05	370
8. Norway	1,912	1865–9	6.65	287
9. Sweden	2,713	1861–9	12.64	215
10. Italy	1,100	1895–9	4.06	271
		1861–9	4.22	261
11. Japan	876	1874–9	11.88	74
12. United States	3,580	1834–43	7.56	474
13. Canada	2,507	1870–4	4.94	508
14. Australia	2,023	1900–4	2.18	930
		1861–9	2.66	760

Source: S. Kuznets, *Economic Growth of Nations*, Cambridge, Harvard University Press, 1971, p. 24.
[1] Dates in parentheses are conjectural.
[2] In 1936 per capita income in the Federal Republic and pre-World War II territory differed by only 2 per cent.

tion increase led to increase of agricultural production by making it possible to increase acreage. It would seem that these changes did not affect the subsistence level of income since at any given time, there was a well defined relationship between population and output which made the subsistence income level a stable equilibrium.

When did Western Europe break away from the low income equilibrium? This is not known precisely, but one possible scenario is as follows. Up to the end of the Middle Ages, income was at subsistence levels; there was a built-in economic mechanism which restored a temporarily displaced income to its original level. Then the economy broke away from this mechanism, and income started to increase, although the increase was so slow and uneven that it does not qualify as modern economic growth. By the time modern economic growth actually began, however, the level of income had become substantially higher than mere subsistence.

It would seem then that in the case of economic development in Western Europe, there was a long period of transition—transition from the period of subsistence income to the beginning of modern economic growth. In Britain, for example, if it can be assumed that the economy broke away from the low income equilibrium towards the end of the Middle Ages, about 200 years must have passed before modern economic growth began. In contrast, there was no such lengthy transition period in Japanese economic development. What this implies is that if it is possible to measure the rate of growth from the time when the economy began to move away from subsistence income to the present, then Japanese economic growth will appear much higher because of the absence of the long transition period experienced in Western countries. The four century path of Britain was telescoped into one century for Japan.

POPULATION GROWTH

Population had remained stable at the level of about 30 million throughout the final 150 years of the Tokugawa period, but began to increase soon after the Meiji Restoration of 1868. Annual growth during the 1870s was somewhere around 0.5 per cent, increasing gradually in the next five decades. It peaked in the 1920s at 1.4 per cent and then declined to the level of 1.0 per cent in the 1960s, though the downward trend was temporarily interrupted during the baby boom in the late 1940s. The rate of population growth in the modern period as a whole has averaged about 1.1 per cent per annum.

Compared with population growth during the period of modern economic growth in Western countries, the Japanese rate is relatively low, but the pressure created even by this rate of population growth was greater in Japan's case because of the unfavourable ratio of population to available land. As shown in Table 1, Australia, the United States, and Canada—the offshoots of Western Europe—recorded much higher growth, and a few Western European countries about the same rate as Japan. But these countries did not face population pressure as heavy as in Japan, for the offshoots of Western Europe had frontier land which served as a safety valve.

Although much of the growing population in Japan was absorbed into gainful employment, since more and more workers were needed to support the expanding economy, not all could be fully absorbed. A percentage of the working population was continually unemployed, or forced into menial work. The increase in open and disguised unemployment during times of economic down-swing became an important source of social discontent, and it is sometimes argued that this was an important factor in the military expansion to the Chinese Continent.

The large number of small companies that characterized the Japanese economy of this period was, in large measure, the result of a relative abundance of labour. Since the increase in the labour force was too rapid for the large firms to absorb completely, many workers had to eke out a living under deplorable working conditions. The existence of this labour force made it possible for small firms which were inferior in capital, technology, and management, to co-exist with the large firms.[3] It is generally considered that the period of labour abundance ended in the early 1960s,[4] but compared with other developed countries, Japan still appears to be a labour abundant country. Even today, there are numerous small shops and restaurants that do not charge customers for home deliveries, and many small manufacturing firms producing simple, but labour-intensive products. To a certain extent, similar small enterprises exist in all developed countries; what is unique in Japan is their relatively important position in the economy.

Although population pressure has always been a more serious concern in Japan than in Western countries, it was never as serious as in the developing countries of today. Most of them have experienced annual population increases of more than 2 per cent in the past few decades, with some over 3 per cent. There is no sign, yet, that these rates will drop significantly in the next twenty-five years. Such large increases have caused serious problems and, indeed, population growth has become the most disequilibrating force in the developing countries. In this comparative perspective, the population problem faced by Japan in its developing period seems much less serious.

The rapid population growth of developing countries began to be a problem when the equilibrium between birth and death rates was disturbed by external factors which brought a sharp decline in the death rate. The first disturbance occurred in the early decades of this century when progressive techniques in medical science developed in the West were introduced to developing countries. Still, the effect at this time was relatively modest. A more dramatic effect has occurred in the last few decades when antibiotics, DDT, and other synthetic materials which destroy germs or their carriers were introduced. Japan has also benefited from these fruits of Western scientific progress, but their impact on the death rate has been small. By the time they were introduced, the death rate was already fairly low due to the improvements in nutrition, medicine and hygiene made possible by the past economic development.

DEVELOPMENT WITH OWN RESOURCES

European countries relied heavily on foreign capital during the early decades of industrial development. For example, France relied on British capital in the post-Napoleonic period, Belgium on French capital in the 1830s, and West Germany on French, Belgian and Swiss capital in the 1840s and 1850s. Even Russia, often considered to be the classic example of internally generated development, depended heavily on foreign capital in building railways and modern industries during the Czarist period.[5]

The Japanese experience was quite different. From the Meiji Restoration to the early 1900s, the only major foreign loan was 5 million yen Japan borrowed in 1870 to build the railroad between Tokyo and Yokohama—itself only a small portion of the railroad constructed in the period. Why so little dependence on foreign capital in the Japanese case? For one thing, Japan was not terribly attractive to potential Western investors. The difference in the interest rates between Japan and the West was not large enough, and the small difference which did exist could be easily wiped out by the on-going devaluation of the yen. Furthermore, there were no extractive industries in Japan to serve the Western market. Conversely, Japan was also cautious about borrowing foreign capital, having witnessed the unhappy experiences of Egypt and Turkey which had mismanaged foreign capital and thus invited foreign intervention.[6]

The situation in the early 1900s was quite different, and Japan needed capital desperately. At the same time, European investors became more willing to invest in Japan, for after the gold standard was adopted in 1897 and the exchange rate stabilized, there was no exchange risk in investing in Japan. The Anglo-Japanese Treaty of 1902 and the victory in the war with Russia also served to increase Japan's credibility as an investment risk. From around 1904, foreign capital began to surge into Japan, and in 1913, foreign capital in Japan amounted to about 2 billion yen (about $1 billion and about a quarter of the GNP for the same year).

There is no question but that foreign borrowing in this period was necessary for the Japanese economy. It is important to note, however, that it was not directly related to industrial development. About 85 per cent of foreign borrowing was done by the government, which used an important part of the funds acquired to finance the Russo-Japanese War. Furthermore, the period in which Japan was indebted to foreign countries was short. After World War I began in 1914, large surpluses in the balance of payments during the war period made Japan a new creditor country. In the intervening years before the Pacific War, Japan maintained its position as net creditor.

Also striking is the cautious approach taken to direct foreign investment. Japan, of course, was not completely free from the effects of multi-national expansion by American and European enterprises. Already in the early 1900s, foreign firms manufacturing electrical machinery (such as Siemens, General Electric, and Westinghouse), had begun to invest in Japan.[7] In the remaining pre-war years, there was a continuous rise in the amount of direct investment. By the mid-1930s, Shell, Nestlé, IBM, and other multi-nationals had set up operations in Japan.[8] Nevertheless, foreign direct investment amounted to only about 200 million yen (about $60 million) at that time.

One might argue that the age of multi-national enterprises did not really begin until the post-war period. Although this is not quite correct in view of the multinational spread in the pre-war period (even if this view is accepted only for the sake of argument), the place occupied by multi-national enterprises in the post-war Japanese economy continued to be small. Originally, the Japanese policy was to prohibit direct foreign investment; if an investment was approved, it was an exceptional measure. This policy was somewhat modified later on, and various concrete steps were taken to liberalize direct foreign investment, especially after Japan joined the OECD (Organization for Economic Cooperation and Development) in 1964. Yet, even today, barriers to investment in Japan remain high.

Since direct investment bestows various benefits on the host country, Japanese policy may not always seem justifiable. In the present-day context, it is sometimes argued that multi-national enterprises are the best hope for industrial revolution and economic development in the Third World. This argument may become more convincing if one remembers the positive effects of regional diversification of industry within a country on production and income in an area where new factories are built. In the United States, for example, corporate migration to the South was an important reason for the rise of industrial production and the increase of wages in that part of the country. Since there is no intrinsic difference in economic impacts between regional diversification and multi-national spread, the same case can be made for direct foreign investment.

This argument did not convince Japanese leaders, however, for although there is no difference in economic impact between foreign and domestic investments, they have quite different cultural implications. For example, an American company may have factories in a number of countries and thus qualify as a multi-national enterprise, yet its language and culture are basically Anglo-Saxon. For Japan to have allowed foreign multi-nationals to increase their position in the economy would have meant adaptation to foreign culture to such an extent as to considerably weaken its cultural identity. This was, of course, repulsive to the nationalistic Japanese leaders who wanted economic development to take place within the Japanese cultural setting. To them, the agent of economic development had to be 'Japanese' corporations–Japanese in the sense that the cultural base was Japanese.

Technology was the one thing in the West which Japan needed desperately for its industrialization. Machinery which incorporated the most recent technological improvements was imported; foreign technicians were invited to Japan; many Japanese went abroad to get training and education; and, if technology was patented, Japanese corporations drew up licensing agreements for its use in Japan. Despite its world position, Japan has continued to be a heavy borrower of technology from the West, as is reflected in the large deficits in the balance of technology trade.[9] Throughout the course of industrial progress, Japan has concentrated on applying the basic technologies developed in the West to the Japanese situation rather than producing them on its own.[10]

Advocates of multi-national enterprises would argue that if investment is allowed freely, it will be accompanied by the introduction of new technology and will contribute to technological progress in the host country. This, however, is not the only way to introduce technology from abroad. The Japanese approach was to 'unbundle' the package of technology and capital which direct investment would imply, and to borrow technology alone, with no strings attached. In general, this approach can work only if the domestic capital market can raise the necessary capital, and if sufficient entrepreneurship is forthcoming. And if it does work, the conflict between industrial development and cultural preservation can be minimized.

TRADITIONAL SETTING

Industrialization is basically incompatible with traditional society since it requires new institutions and values. The place of production must be moved to a factory, for example, and the comprehension of the principles of industrial technology necessitates the development of rational thinking. Yet, in Japanese industrialization, the break with traditional society was far from complete. Many traditional values and institutions were retained during the course of industrial progress. Even today, remnants of traditional society can be observed.

One reason for this is obviously that the post-traditional period was short in Japan. In contrast with Britain, which had a transition period of about two centuries, the transition accomplished in the Meiji era was so rapid that it now seems to have been almost non-existent. Furthermore, since growth was rapid, a level of development comparable to that in the West was reached quite soon. If anything, there was not enough time for society to digest this enormous economic growth, and therefore, many traditional social institutions survived this period intact.[11]

This is not, however, the only reason for the prolonged life of traditional Japanese society. It is important to note the conscious efforts of the Japanese government to preserve certain traditional values and institutions. Complete preservation of tradition may have been clearly inimical to the establishment of a democratic society, but the goal of the government in the pre-war period was to create a militarily strong country, and for this purpose it was expedient to preserve a certain part of traditional society. For example, the traditional family, which has played an important role in Japanese modernization, was retained and promoted by the government as an institution useful for achieving its goal.[12]

The traditional family provided a basis for the new economic institutions necessary for industrialization. In fact, the Japanese company resembles the traditional family in many respects. This point should not be stretched too far, but just as there is a certain amount of truth in characterizing the United States as the country of 'rags to riches', it is not completely unreasonable to characterize the Japanese company as a family-like institution.[13]

Like children in a family, employees remain in the same company until they reach retirement age. For the management to fire them is as rare as for a father to disown his child. In the same way that age determines position within a family, it also plays an important role in determining one's position in the corporate hierarchy. Promotion is also a function of age. In major Japanese companies, most chief executive officers are in their sixties and seventies. The parent-child relationship is translated into a fictive kinship relationship referred to as *oyabun-kobun*. In a factory, a foreman is the *oyabun* and his subordinates, *kobun*. The primary job of the *oyabun* is, of course, to train and supervise his *kobun*, but it is his equally important duty to look after their emotional and social needs.

As with the family, fellow employees in one's company constitute one's primary social group. A person's close friends all work in the same company, and various recreational activities are organized by the company. Employees usually live in company housing, and their wives know each other well. Thus, if a Japanese man were asked what he does for a living, the typical reply would be that he works for such-and-such company. If the same question were asked in the West, the typical answer would be 'I am an accountant', 'I am an engineer', etc. This type of reply does not come from the Japanese until he is asked what he does in the company. His function within the company is not his primary identification, since it is dictated by the needs of the company at any particular point in time. It is in this sense that a typical Japanese employee is often called a 'company man'.

Interpersonal harmony is greatly emphasized and employees are expected to be loyal to the company. Their loyalty is, in turn, rewarded by the management which pays close attention to their welfare. This paternalistic relationship has been preserved despite the great rise in

›f trade unions in the post-war period. Unlike in the ere is no sharp conflict between management and a Japanese company. If a company does better in the current year than in the previous, management makes sure that workers get pay raises or bonuses.

Evidence disproving the analogy of the company to the family is in no short supply—but the fact remains that various features which look peculiar to Western observers (such as group loyalty, emphasis on group performance, seniority, etc.) were born when industry was grafted upon traditional society. However far-fetched the analogy may appear, those features can best be explained when the company is regarded as a fictive family.

One implication of the Japanese experience refutes the necessity of imitating Western society in order to carry out industrialization. Democratic values and institutions were irrelevant in the Japanese case. For a considerable period of time after development started, traditional values and institutions were preserved. There is no necessity for economic organizations (such as companies) to be purely economic organizations; in the Japanese model, they work best when they fulfil the social as well as the economic needs of workers. Furthermore, it is possible to recognize in traditional society a basis for industrialization and economic development. Because social structures often prove to be resistant to rapid change, industrialization may be more successful when traditional values and institutions are maintained.

THE ROLE OF THE GOVERNMENT

The Japanese government was much more extensively involved in economic development than were the governments of Western countries. In the early Meiji era, the government pioneered industrialization by setting up model factories and introducing machine technology from the West. Most of the model factories were transferred to the private sector in the 1880s, but state enterprises remained important throughout the pre-war period in the production of iron and steel, machinery, and armaments. Furthermore, the government took major responsibility for the construction of railroads, communications, and other types of overhead capital. These government activities are reflected in the relatively large size of government investment. Rosovsky writes that 'government was the largest and most important investor in the economy. Its share of domestic capital formation never averaged less than 40 per cent, and it was only rarely that low.'[14]

Government influence was not confined to direct involvement in the economy. It also gave subsidies and incentives to promote development of certain industries, provided heavy industry with protection from foreign competition in the 1920s and 1930s, and aided the *zaibatsu* in establishing a dominant position in the economy.

In the post-war period, the nature of government involvement changed, yet it continued to take an active role.[15] Until the early 1960s, the government controlled imports by quotas and exchange controls. It had an important bearing on the structure of industry by limiting the accessibility of foreign technology to a small number of firms, and by controlling plant construction and expansion on the pretext of avoiding 'excess competition'. Furthermore, by channelling investment funds of government and quasi-governmental financial institutions to industries which were considered to have high growth potential, the government shaped the pattern of industrial development.

The main reason for the involvement of the Meiji government in economic development is related to the way in which it came to power.[16] Its leaders were dissatisfied with the social and economic conditions in the late Tokugawa period and had spearheaded the Restoration movement to establish a new society. The new government they subsequently created was not intended to preserve the *status quo*, but was rather the agent through which they aimed to carry out certain modernization goals.

One might argue that it would have been sufficient for the nation's leaders to have simply designated the direction in which the economy should evolve without directly involving the government in the process of development. The social and economic conditions the Meiji government inherited were, however, too unfavourable to rely solely on private initiative. The merchant class had become overly accustomed to feudal protection and had ceased to be an innovating force. In general, merchants were reluctant to risk capital in new ventures. The capital market was fragmented to a considerable extent along family lines, making it unlikely that sufficient private capital could be mobilized to build a nationwide system of communications and transportation or to construct large-scale factories for shipbuilding, iron and steel, or other modern industries. Under such circumstances, it was imperative for the government to take measures to enlighten the public about the power of modern industry, to develop nationwide financial institutions, to promote joint-stock companies, and to assume the primary responsibility for projects which required large capital investment.[17]

The gap between what the government wanted and what the private sector could accomplish was made acute by the threat of Western imperialism. Having seen how Japan's neighbour, China, had been victimized by Western Powers, Meiji leaders had become convinced of the need for military modernization and the build-up of the supporting economy. If Japan were to avoid China's fate, both military modernization and economic development had to be carried out immediately. Since the response of the private sector was expected to be slow and limited in scope, the government was forced to play an active role as educator, institutional innovator, and financier.

To a people accustomed to a democratic system of government (one which reflects the views of the public), the idea of a government ruling the public by independent goals would be objectionable, but given their experience with the feudal Tokugawa regime, such a system was readily acceptable to the Japanese. In fact, it is only recently that the Japanese public has become more conscious of its political rights under the post-war democracy. In the Meiji period, it was nothing unusual for the government to establish new goals for the country and direct the public to attain them; in fact, it was in accordance with a long established tradition of the supremacy of a governing élite.[18] In a way, the public expected the government to take initiatives, and were basically willing to follow its guidance.

The dominating influence of the government persisted throughout the pre-war period. When there was no urgency for military build-up (e.g. the early 1920s), the government loosened its control on the economy somewhat, but its interventionist nature never changed. In the 1930s, when military build-up was renewed with great intensity, the government gradually replaced the market mechanism with a 'command economy'. In the post-war period, with the military backbone of the country crushed, the political system became more democratic, but it was only slowly that the concept of democratic government took root in Japanese society. Meanwhile, the supremacy of the government remained unchallenged. This made it possible for the government to assume actively the helm of reconstruction from war-time devastation to subsequent post-war economic prosperity.

PRICE INCREASE

Japanese economic development took place within an inflationary setting. From the mid-1880s to the mid-1930s, although there were some ups and downs, consumer prices increased about 4.5 times, an annual rate of slightly over 2 per cent. The pace of increase quickened from the mid-1930s, and then developed into the hyperinflation of the early post-war years. By the early 1950s, prices had stabilized, but the rate of increase in the following years became even faster than in the pre-war period: from 1950 to 1973, the consumer price index increased slightly over three times. Even if the war and immediate post-war years are excluded, the rate of increase has been much faster in Japan than in Western countries.[19] In the relatively stable period of the mid-1880s to the mid-1930s, prices increased in Japan about twice as fast as in the United States or Britain.

Did the price increase stimulate economic growth? Since the public had certain illusions about the current value of money, the answer to the question must be 'yes'. Those who hold the Keynesian view will argue that since the initial impact of inflation is an increase in the price of output while wages and interests remain constant, inflation increases profits. Increased profits subsequently increase total savings by redistributing income in favour of capitalist entrepreneurs who have a higher propensity to save, and in turn, stimulate investment by raising its rate of return. On the other hand, those who accept the quantity theory of money will argue that, since inflation distributes income from the holders of cash balance to the government which issues money (that is, inflation imposes 'tax' on holdings of money), inflation stimulates growth only as long as the government uses the additional income for investment. Whichever view is accepted, inflation is to be considered a favourable factor for growth.[20]

Although inflation accompanied economic growth, and even contributed somewhat, it is far from accurate to say that the government has consistently pursued an inflationary policy. At various times, the government has made serious efforts to keep down the price increase, and in two periods it resorted to deflationary measures in order to bring down the price level. Sharp deflationary measures were taken to restore the convertibility of paper notes (in 1881–6), and to maintain the exchange rate from before World War I (in 1920–31). These deflationary measures prevented prices from eventually getting out of hand.

One might criticize the deflationary measures of the 1920s on the grounds that they were unrealistic. During World War I, Japan experienced a large surplus in the balance of payments which led to an increased money supply, and consequently, a price increase of approximately 250 per cent. It is quite conceivable that the price level after the war was too high to maintain the original exchange rate, so it may actually have been better to let the rate depreciate. Instead, efforts were made to maintain the original rate by deflationary measures and by reducing the price level to that of the United States and Britain. The government finally achieved this objective in January 1931 when the gold standard was reinstituted at the pre-war exchange rate. Unfortunately, however, this demanded sacrifice within the economy and made the 1920s a gloomy decade of high unemployment and many bankruptcies. In retrospect, maintenance of the original exchange rate after major economic changes had occurred seems to have been not only impractical, but harmful.

Nevertheless, Japanese monetary authorities can be given credit for having had the courage and determination to take deflationary measures. They can be favourably contrasted with monetary authorities in developing countries today who often badly mismanage monetary affairs. In these countries (since there is no need to back up the issue of paper notes with bullion or hard currency) monetary authority tends to become lax on money supply, and, thus, contributes to inflation. A fixed exchange rate is a potential check on inflation, but once it starts, devaluation is often the only way out, because measures to reduce the price level become politically unpalatable. A slow rate of inflation may have some positive effects, but beyond a certain rate (possibly a few per cent), inflation is more likely to be harmful because of the economic instability created. Japanese leaders perhaps made too much fuss about maintaining the fixed exchange rate, but this policy at least had the virtue of ensuring monetary responsibility.

In the post-war period, there was a peculiar development in the relation between price movement and the exchange rate. According to the theory of purchasing power parity, if Japan wants to maintain the dollar-yen exchange rate, its prices must change at the same rate as prices in the United States. That is, the fixed exchange rate is inconsistent with a disparate price movement between the two countries. What is puzzling in the Japanese case is that, although the consumer price index increased much faster than in the United States in the post-war period, the same exchange rate was maintained until almost the end of 1971, when the yen was revalued instead of devalued!

One answer to this puzzle is that high growth caused divergence in the price movement in Japan between tradable (goods) and non-tradable (services) sectors. After surplus labour began to disappear in the late 1950s, high growth pushed prices up in the non-tradable sector where, because of the labour intensive nature of production, there was little room for the introduction of cost-saving technology, and consequently, the consumer price index (which includes prices in the non-tradable sector) increased. On the other hand, prices in the tradable sector (which enter into the balance of payments and thus influence the exchange rate) increased much more slowly in Japan than in the United States, making it possible not only to maintain the fixed exchange rate, but eventually to revalue the yen in the 1970s.[21]

1. S. Kuznets, *Modern Economic Growth: Rate, Structure, and Spread*, New Haven, Yale University Press, 1966, Chapter 1.

2. K. Ohkawa and H. Rosovsky, *Japanese Economic Growth: Trend Acceleration in the Twentieth Century*, Stanford, Stanford University Press, 1973.

3. Arisawa Hiromi, *Nihon Kogyo Tosei Ron* [Discourse on regulation of Japanese industry], Tokyo, Yuhikaku, 1937.

4. *Keizai Hakusho* mentions labour shortage for the first time in its 1961 report.

5. D. Landes, 'Japan and Europe: Contrasts in Industrialization', in W. Lockwood (ed.), *The State and Economic Enterprise in Japan*, Princeton, Princeton University Press, 1965, pp. 95–7.

6. J. Dower (ed.), *Origins of the Modern Japanese State: Selected Writings of E. H. Norman*, New York, Pantheon Books, 1975, p. 223.

7. W. Lockwood, *The Economic Development of Japan: Growth and Structural Change*, expanded edition, Princeton, Princeton University Press, 1968, pp. 322–3.

8. Ministry of International Trade and Industry, *Gaishi-kei Kigyo: sono Jittai to Eikyo* [Foreign-affiliated firms: their realties and influences], Tokyo, Printing Office, Ministry of Finance, 1968, p. 15.

9. For Japan's borrowing of technology from abroad in the post-war period, see M. Peck, 'Technology', in H. Patrick and H. Rosovsky (eds.), *Asia's New Giant*, Washington, The Brookings Institution, 1976.

10. For the nature of Japanese technological progress, see Hoshino Yoshiro, *Nihon no Gijutsu Kakushin* [Technological progress in Japan], Tokyo, Keiso Shobo, 1965, Chapter 7.

11. Nakayama Ichiro, *The Industrialization of Japan*, Honolulu, University Press of Hawaii, 1965, p. 38.

12. Sakata Yoshio, 'Nihon Kindaika no Shuppatsu to Tenkai' [The 'Take Off' and Expansion of Japan's Modernization], *The Jinbun Gakuho*, March 1970.

13. The following discussion on the Japanese company and family is based on the concluding chapter of J. Abbeglen, *Japanese Factory*, Glencoe, Illinois, Free Press, 1958.

14. H. Rosovsky, *Capital Formation in Japan*, Glencoe, Illinois, Free Press, 1961, p. 23.

15. For the role of the government in the post-war economy, see P. Trezise, 'Politics, Government, and Economic Growth in Japan', in H. Patrick and H. Rosovsky (eds.), *Asia's New Giant*, Washington, The Brookings Institution, 1976.

16. It might be suggested that, in general, the more backward a country is, the greater the role of the government in economic development. See A. Gerschenkron in *Economic Backwardness in Historical Perspective*, Cambridge, Harvard University Press, 1962.

17. Dower (ed.), op. cit., p. 221, and Lockwood, op. cit., pp. 505–7.

18. Dower (ed.), op. cit., p. 154.

19. K. Ohkawa, *et al.*, *Prices: Estimates of Long-Term Economic Statistics of Japan since 1868, Vol. 8*, Tokyo, Toyo Keizai Shinposha, 1967, p. 12.

20. For a more detailed discussion on inflation and economic growth, see Harry Johnson, 'Is Inflation the Inevitable Price of Rapid Development or a Retarding Factor in Economic Growth?', *Malayan Economic Review*, April 1966.

21. For further discussion on this point, see R. McKinnon, 'Monetary Theory and Controlled Flexibility in the Foreign Exchanges', Essays in International Finance, No. 84, Department of Economics, Princeton University, April 1971.

III
Trade and Development

TRADE EXPANSION

JAPANESE development did not take place in isolation: international trade was inextricably interwoven with development. In fact, it is difficult to conceive that without trade the high standard of living Japan enjoys today could be maintained. This chapter first treats trade as one facet of development and discusses trade patterns and their changes, and then considers the impact of trade on development. Chapter I looked at Japanese development from the historical perspective, and Chapter II from the international perspective. This chapter looks at Japanese development from yet another perspective—that of international trade.

The Tokugawa period was a period of relative isolation. Foreign trade with the Dutch and Chinese was limited to the port of Nagasaki, and with the Koreans to Tsushima, an island in the Korean Straits. Trade volume was restricted and small, however, and had little influence on the economic and social affairs of the country. Thus, the period from the mid-seventeenth century to the mid-nineteenth century may be considered one of virtual seclusion.

A dramatic change in Japan's foreign policy took place in 1854 when Matthew C. Perry, an American Commodore, threatened siege of the city of Edo and forced the shogunate to sign a treaty called the Treaty of Kanagawa. It stipulated that two ports were to be opened to American ships for provisions; that shipwrecked Americans were to be well-treated; and that an American consular agent was to be allowed to reside in Japan. It was not, however, until 1859 that the Western Powers succeeded in opening actual trade with Japan. A year earlier, the Tokugawa shogunate was persuaded by the first American Ambassador, Townsend Harris, to sign commercial treaties with the West—the treaties known collectively in Japan as the 'Treaties with Five Nations'.

In the first few years, exports increased rapidly. Silk was most popular among the goods bought by Western merchants. Difficulties involved in increasing the silk supply and a variety of political reasons[1] caused exports, however, to stagnate in the remaining several years of the Tokugawa period. It was not until the early Meiji period that trade expansion became a built-in feature of the Japanese economy.

As shown in Table 3, the growth of trade was spectacular in the succeeding period. From the mid-1870s to the mid-1930s, both exports and imports increased at an annual rate of about 7 per cent. This rate was twice to three times as fast as the growth rate of world trade in the same period. From the late 1930s to the mid-1940s, as a consequence of the Pacific War, trade sharply declined. Then, in the post-war years, as the Japanese economy recovered from wartime destruction and dislocation, trade expanded again. Nevertheless, the pre-war level of trade was not reached until the late 1950s, a point which should be contrasted with the recovery of other economic indicators (such as industrial production, agricultural production and per capita income) which had returned to the pre-war level by the early 1950s.

This late recovery of trade was due to the difficulties Japan faced in exporting. Silk, a major export commodity in the pre-war period, lost its importance due to the appearance of nylon. Cotton textiles, another major export in the pre-war period, faced trade barriers erected by newly emergent countries which had decided to pursue import-substitution industrialization. China, the major market in

TABLE 3

Export and Import Quantity Index, Terms of Trade, and Ratios of Exports and Imports to GNP

	Export Quantity Index	*Import Quantity Index*	*Terms of Trade*	*Exports/ National Income*	*Imports/ National Income*
1873–7	1.4	1.6	111.3	4.5	5.1
1878–82	2.0	2.4	129.2	4.2	4.6
1883–7	2.8	2.6	137.9	5.0	3.9
1888–92	4.5	4.9	131.3	6.3	6.1
1893–7	5.7	7.9	135.4	7.4	8.6
1898–1902	8.4	11.8	134.8	11.8	12.3
1903–7	11.6	16.4	144.9	13.2	15.3
1908–12	15.5	17.7	125.2	13.3	14.4
1913–17	26.1	21.5	110.0	20.2	16.9
1918–22	26.8	31.2	112.2	17.3	19.0
1923–7	32.2	43.4	121.3	16.9	21.2
1928–32	44.4	45.2	104.2	16.5	18.1
1933–7	73.5	53.0	76.1	21.6	22.9
1948–52	19.2	22.8	82.7	7.1	11.1
1953–7	50.2	56.9	88.4	10.7	15.6
1958–62	99.0	101.1	97.7	12.0	13.6
1963–7	219.3	193.6	96.4	10.9	10.7
1968–72	471.4	367.4	98.6	11.5	9.9

Source: Economic Planning Agency, *Nihon no Keizai Tokei* [Japanese economic statistics], Volume 1, and Office of the Prime Minister, *Japan Statistical Yearbook*.

[1] 1960 = 100 for the export and import quantity index.

[2] Terms of trade is defined as the ratio of export price index to import price index. The base year for both indexes is 1960.

the pre-war period, became a communist state and restricted its trade with capitalist countries. Despite these difficulties, however, Japan succeeded in creating new markets and new export goods by the late 1950s. In the next decade, the growth of exports continued at an annual rate of increase of about 17 per cent, with the volume of exports increasing about five times. This rapid export expansion continued until the oil crisis of late 1973. Imports were initially constrained by the lack of foreign exchange, but as exports increased, this constraint was eased, and imports also increased rapidly in the post-war period.

The rapid expansion of exports over a long period of time was made possible because new export commodities were created before the old ones began to decline. This pattern is shown in Figure 1. At first, Japan exported silk, a primary product in the sense that it was produced by farm households. Around 1900, while the export of silk was growing, Japan completed the import-substitution stage of textile production and began to export textiles to China. World War I was a tremendous blessing to Japanese textile exports. Britain, the dominant supplier of textiles until the war, was forced to withdraw from the Asian scene, for wartime dislocation and the German naval blockade of the British Isles made it impossible for Britain to maintain supply links with Asia. Japanese textiles moved with great vigour into the vacuum created. After the war, Britain tried to regain the lost markets, but without much success. In the Chinese market, for example, Japan had by then consolidated its position and was able to block British re-entry. Britain was more successful in South-East Asia and India, but even there, Japanese textiles penetrated increasingly in the late 1920s and the 1930s. Around 1930, textile exports surpassed silk exports for the first time, and became a major foreign exchange earner.

Textiles were soon joined by various other light industrial goods, and together they represent the second product cycle in Figure 1. After being surpassed by textile exports, silk exports declined sharply due to the depression in the West and the invention of nylon. In place of silk, light industrial products rose in significance to become the propelling force of Japanese exports. Garments, plastic products, and other labour intensive miscellaneous manufactured

FIGURE 1
Changes in Leading Exports over Time

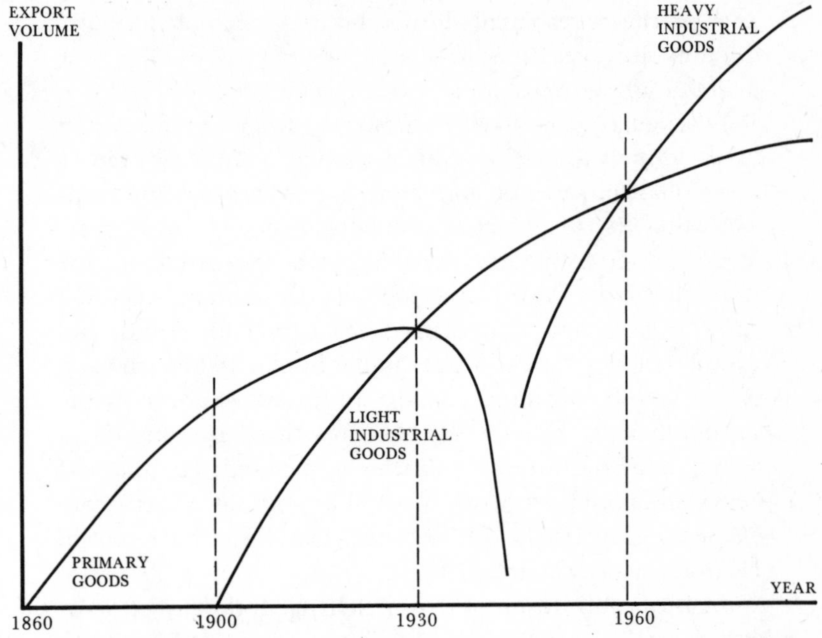

goods became important, especially in the early post-war years when they were exported to the United States and other Western countries where labour costs were much higher than in Japan. It was at the early part of this stage of development that the phrase 'made in Japan' became synonymous with poor quality products.

Around 1960, the export of light industrial products was surpassed by that of heavy industrial products. As discussed in Chapter I, heavy industry became more important as Japan developed, becoming particularly vital in the 1930s when a heavy industrialization programme was deliberately fostered by the government in preparation for imminent war. The push towards heavy industry was further accelerated in the war years. In the post-war economic recovery this industrial imbalance was corrected, to a certain extent, but there was still a considerable emphasis on heavy industry. Under the protection and financial assistance of the government, heavy industry expanded its production to eventually become the centre of Japanese manufacturing industry.

For many years, heavy industry had been predominant in the domestic market, but in the late 1950s it began to establish itself also as an export industry. Steel and ships were the first major exports followed by electronic products. The first electronic product to be exported was the transistor radio, which was followed by the tape recorder and the black and white television in the early 1960s and by the colour television later in the decade. When cars and synthetic fibres joined the list of major exports in the second half of the 1960s, the growth of the export of heavy industrial products further accelerated. The share of heavy industrial products in total exports increased from 50 per cent in 1960, to 65 per cent in 1965, 76 per cent in 1970 and 83 per cent in 1973.

As the composition of exports changed, the direction of exports also changed. In the first period (1860–1900), Japanese exports went mostly to Western countries. This is the period when Japan exported silk and other primary products to the West. In the second period (1900–30), the developing areas, especially China, became important Japanese markets while primary exports to the West continued. From the second period onward, there was no great change in the direction of exports, although the Western share in total exports varied. (It declined, for example, in the 1930s as Japan became isolated from the West, and increased in the 1950s and 1960s when Japan aimed its export drive at high income countries.) The type of goods exported, however, changed. In the third period (1930–60), light industrial goods have gradually dropped out, and heavy industrial products have come to dominate Japanese exports to both the West and the developing areas.

As exports changed in composition and direction, changes also took place in imports. Imports of consumption goods in the first period occupied an important position, but lost importance as domestic production of consumption goods (particularly textiles) increased. In the second and third periods, intermediate goods, capital goods and primary products (cotton, iron ore, food, etc.) became the principal Japanese imports. Then, as Japanese industrialization further progressed in the direction of heavy industry, primary products alone became the principal Japanese imports. Conceivably, a next period (that is, the fifth period) will be a period in which light industrial products become important in total imports, though clearly not as important as primary products. In the early 1970s, when light industrial goods were imported from Korea, Taiwan and other developing countries, there was some indication that a fifth period would begin shortly, but because of the oil crisis of late 1973, its arrival has been delayed.

As the composition of imports changed, the sources of imports also shifted. Britain, which had been the major supplier of textiles in the Meiji period, lost its relative importance when textile imports were replaced by domestic production. The United States, on the other hand, became important as a supplier of both primary products and capital goods. Developing countries which possess natural resources have gained in importance, especially in the fourth period, since primary products have become increasingly important as Japanese imports. In the future, these countries will become even more important as the source of imports, while the United States' share will decline.

These export and import trends reflect changes in the relationship between Japan and foreign countries. In the first period, Japan imported consumption goods from the West and exported primary products back to the West. The relationship between Japan and the West was, in general, complementary. Japan's relationship with the developing areas, however, was one of substitution, since their economic structures were basically similar. In the second and third periods, Japan's relationship with the West became both complementary and competitive. It was complementary in the sense that Japan exported primary goods and light industrial goods, and imported capital and intermediate goods. It was competitive in that Japan competed with some Western countries (Britain in particular) in selling textiles and other light industrial goods. Japan's relationship with the developing areas became complementary in this period since it exported industrial goods and imported primary products. The composition of Japan's exports changed over time; the early dominance of consumption goods gave way to heavy industrial goods as these areas pursued import substitution industrialization in the field of consumption goods.

In the fourth period (1960 to the present), Japan's relationship with the developing areas has remained constant, but that with the West has been more competitive than complementary. As a result of capital accumulation, the factor proportion[2] in Japan became similar to that in the West, and consequently, exports of light industrial goods have lost significance. The heavy industrial goods which have replaced them are precisely those in which the West has vested interest. The strain on a relationship such as this would be eased if (as in the case of the United States) a Western country could export primary products, or if income in both countries rises relatively fast. Otherwise, the relationship will remain competitive and will contain potential conflicts. The difficulties Japan faces today in exporting steel, colour television sets and cars to the West are best understood within this framework.[3]

TRADE MODELS

The pattern of Japanese trade is so complex that it is necessary to resort to the theory of international trade as an explanatory construct. Trade models proposed thus far have been built upon rather simplistic assumptions, but still, they bring out certain features in the pattern of trade in Japan that might otherwise go unnoticed. In this section, three major trade models are described in the simplest terms possible; then, the ways in which they can be used to explain the Japanese trade pattern are discussed.[4]

The first model is the Ricardian model. It assumes that labour is the only factor of production and that there are only two commodities and two countries in the world. The price ratio of the two commodities is determined by relative labour productivity—the ratio of the labour productivity of one commodity to that of the other. If the price ratio of one country differs from that of the other, trade between the two countries can take place. The first exports the commodity in which it has relatively high labour productivity—the commodity in which it has comparative advantage—and imports the commodity in which it has relatively low labour productivity. The goods exported by the first country are the goods imported by the second, and vice versa.

Another model is the Heckscher-Ohlin model, which is built upon three basic assumptions: (a) that there are two factors of production (labour and capital); (b) that there are only two commodities and two countries in the world; and (c) that production technology is the same for the two countries. When trade takes place, the model predicts that the country where capital is relatively abundant (i.e., abundant relative to the capital endowment in the second country) will export the capital intensive product and the country where labour is relatively abundant will export the labour intensive product. The two factors of production usually discussed in connexion with this model are capital and labour, but they can be any two. For example, they can be non-reproducible (land, including natural resources) and reproducible inputs (some aggregate of labour and capital). The model predicts that, in such a case, the country abundat in the non-reproducible input case, the country abundant in the non-reproducible input will export the resource intensive product and that the country abundant in the reproducible input will export the 'capital-labour' intensive product.

Those who are attracted to the theoretical beauty of the Heckscher-Ohlin model argue that differences in technology can be dealt with within the framework of the model by considering technical knowledge as an input. Thus, a country like the United States will export technologically advanced products (technology intensive products) because it has a relatively great abundance of technical knowledge. This may stretch interpretation of the model too far, since it assumes categorically that the two countries have the same levels of technology. It seems more reasonable to introduce here the technological gap model which assumes an explicit difference in technology between countries. According to this model, the reason why the United States exports aeroplanes, high quality semiconductors, computers, etc., is that American companies possess new technology not known to companies in other countries. This technological gap may be temporary, but it can be substantial because the new technology may be patented or because the small size of the domestic market for new products makes it difficult for less advanced countries to start production on a substantially large scale and acquire the new technology involved in the production.

Unfortunately, none of the three models adequately explains the Japanese trade pattern. The technological gap model explains fairly well Japan's import of aeroplanes, computers and high quality integrated circuits, but it is a poor explanation of the imports of primary products. In this case, the Heckscher-Ohlin model is a better explanation (if land–including natural resources–is considered as an input). The Heckscher-Ohlin model also explains well the imports of garments, toys and other light industrial goods in the recent period when the factor proportion in Japan changed in favour of capital. It fails, however, to account for the Japanese imports of textiles and machinery in the early modern period; and in this case, the technological gap model seems to be more relevant.

In explaining Japanese export patterns, it likewise seems necessary to adopt an eclectic approach toward the application of models. Japanese exports of garments and other light industrial goods from the early 1930s to the early 1960s, and of silk in the first six decades of the modern period can be explained in terms of the Heckscher-Ohlin model. Japan had a comparative advantage in labour intensive products because wages were relatively low until recently. Exports of textile fabrics to China and other developing countries in the pre-war period are also related to the fact that Japan had a comparative advantage in labour intensive production *vis-à-vis* Britain. (Spinning is not very labour intensive, but weaving is.) Still, the usefulness of the Heckscher-Ohlin model is a qualified one here for it was only after the Japanese textile industry caught up with the technological level of the British that the factor proportion came into play.

The export of electronic products reflects a similar problem. The reason why Japan could export various consumer electronic products in the late 1950s and the early 1960s was that they involved labour intensive production processes. Given the same level of technology in consumer electronics, Japan had comparative advantage in such production over the United States and other high wage countries. But when Hong Kong, Taiwan, Korea and Singapore caught up with Japan in technology, Japan lost the comparative advantage in transistor radios, black and white televisions and other relatively unsophisticated consumer electronic products. The extent to which the Heckscher-Ohlin model can be relied on to explain the exports of such electronic goods is determined by the presence of a technological gap between Japan and its Asian competitors. As soon as the gap closes, the model becomes useful in explaining the decline of Japanese electronics exports.

Neither the Heckscher-Ohlin model nor the technological gap model explains well the rise of the exports of steel, colour television sets and cars—the three major Japanese exports today. Production of these goods is not labour intensive (it is usually considered to employ capital intensive production techniques). Since it cannot be argued that capital is more abundant in Japan than in the West where the bulk of the exports goes, the Heckscher-Ohlin model cannot be used. The technological gap model is also inapplicable, since it is hardly possible to argue that Japan has more advanced technical knowledge with regard to these products. They are relatively old products, and the level of technology required for their production can be considered to be shared by all industrial countries.

The only possible explanation for Japan's export of steel, colour television sets and cars seem to be that Japanese productivity in these products is higher than that in other countries—thus, the Ricardian model applies. If one objects to the Ricardian assumption that labour is the only factor of production, an aggregate input index constructed from labour and capital can be considered as an input, and the model can be salvaged in terms of total factor productivity (productivity of the aggregate input) instead of labour productivity.

A serious difficulty arises in connexion with the Ricardian model, however. The extent of the circularity of the reasoning involved in explaining the actual trade pattern by the Heckscher-Ohlin model or the technological gap model is limited, but the situation is quite different with the Ricardian model. According to this model, the high level of productivity in steel, for example, would be explained by the fact that it is a major export commodity. Clearly the logic is reversed here. If the model is to be useful for predicting future trade patterns, it must be determined whether the productivity of the Japanese steel industry is increasing or decreasing relative to that in other countries.

Even if the productivity trend is known, the problem of its explanation remains. Here, one cannot resort to national characteristics (such as the Japanese work ethic) as an explanation, since not all industries increased productivity uniformly; some became more productive than others. What needs explanation is the increased productivity of steel, cars and colour television sets relative to that of aluminium, electrical appliances (refrigerators, air conditioners, etc.), copper, etc. If this question is to be dealt with satisfactorily, the mental make-up of the entrepreneurs who played an important role in the formative period must be studied along with government policy and industrial history. At this point, it is necessary to leave the neat field of economic theory.

Although the Heckscher-Ohlin model gives a good explanation for why Japan exported garments and labour intensive products in the 1950s and why it began to import the same products in the 1970s, it is a poor model to prescribe an optimal path of a country's exports over the course of development, since its policy prescription is static. If a country is labour abundant, the model recommends that it specialize in the labour intensive product. But this recommendation is hardly acceptable for a country which wants to create a comparative advantage in heavy industrial goods.

During preparation for the first long-term plan of the post-war economy drafted in 1949, there was heated discussion concerning which manufacturing industries should be the focus of exports in the future.[5] Apparently, there were three different views expressed. One view was basically in agreement with the policy prescription of the Heckscher-Ohlin model: since Japan had a comparative advantage in light industrial products, this type of goods should play a central role in Japanese exports. The second was its opposite: although Japan did not have a comparative advantage in heavy industrial goods, the government should take measures to promote heavy industry and create a comparative advantage in heavy industrial goods since the demand for such goods in the world market was expected to rise sharply in the future. The third view was that, since Japan was short of capital, it should not aim at the export of heavy industrial goods; instead, it should make precision machinery the major export in the future.

The Japanese government did not discourage light industry or the precision machinery industry, but it did give top priority in the industrial plan to heavy industry. The protection and subsidy heavy industry received from the government is an important reason for its success in post-war Japan. In the late 1950s, this policy began to bear fruit, and in the 1960s and 1970s, heavy industrial goods became the major Japanese exports. Nevertheless, in the early and mid-1950s, when the outcome of the heavy industrialization policy was still uncertain, the government was criticized by conventional trade theorists. A distinguished Western economist argued, for example, that the Japanese government should stop subsidizing production of cars (an item for which Japan did not have the comparative advantage), and re-allocate the resources tied up in car production to labour intensive industry, where Japan had a comparative advantage. These criticisms were, however, ignored and heavy industrialization was promoted. In retrospect, this was a wise decision, for which the government can be given credit.

This does not imply, however, that heavy industrialization can be promoted in complete disregard of the factor proportion. In the post-war period, many developing countries pursued import-substitution policies and began production of some heavy industrial products but their industrial performance has not been impressive. Especially in heavy industry, the rate of utilization of machinery is low because of the limited size of their domestic market, and consequently the costs of production tend to be high by international standards. Recently, industrial policy has been re-evaluated and the enthusiasm for heavy industry which existed in the early post-war period seems to have dissipated considerably. But since the shift to heavy industry is essential at some stage of industrialization, and can be promoted by government measures, the industrial plan for developing countries cannot be discussed solely from the viewpoint of the factor proportion. The Japanese case suggests that a government can accelerate the shift toward heavy industry by taking appropriate measures, but under what circumstances and at what speed heavy industry should be promoted are questions still not clearly understood. If a government intervenes too early, or on too large a scale, it can actually retard progress.

TRADE AND DEVELOPMENT

There are two opposing views on the relationship between trade and development. The first view is that trade is a 'handmaiden of growth', that is, that economic growth is the cause of trade expansion.[6] The opposite view is that trade is 'an engine of growth'.[7] According to this view, trade expansion is not a passive consequence of economic growth, but is its propelling force. When the relationship is examined in the Japanese context, it is difficult to subscribe to the first view. Undoubtedly, trade expansion was partly a result of economic growth, but to deny it any active role in Japanese economic development does not seem to be correct.

How does trade promote economic development? According to the theory of international trade, trade increases the income of a participating country by making it possible to exchange goods whose production cost is comparatively low for goods whose cost is comparatively high. This can be better explained by using a diagram. In Figure 2, the curve passing through points D, A, and B is the production possibility curve which shows various combina-

FIGURE 2

Gains from Trade

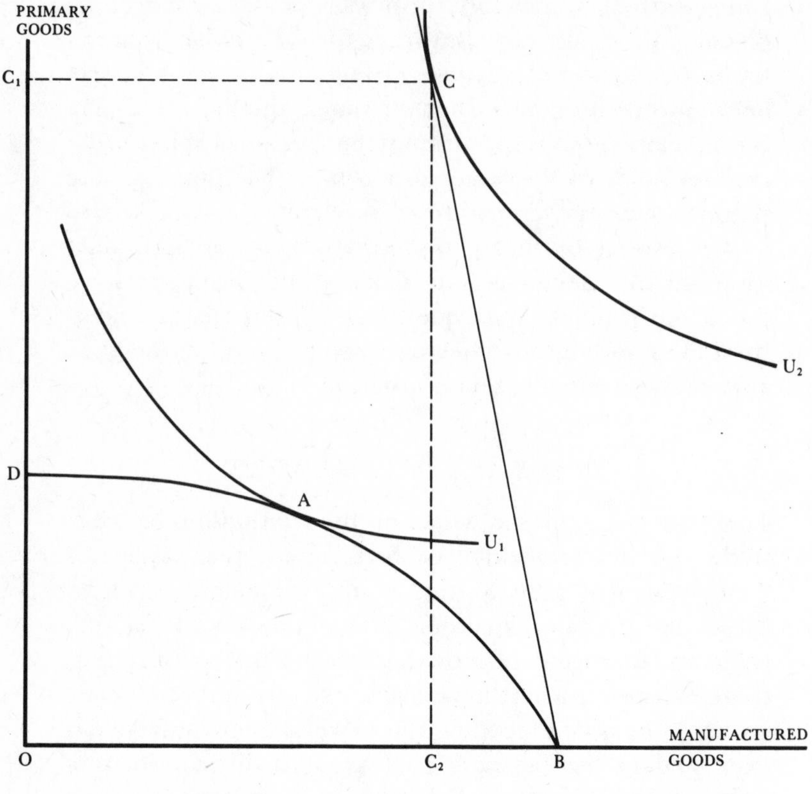

tions of primary and manufactured goods which can be produced with the available quantity of inputs. Curves U_1 and U_2 are social indifference curves, which can be interpreted as representing the standard of living.

Before trade begins, the combination of primary and manufactured goods represented by point A is produced and U_1 (the highest living standard which can be attained given the production possibility curve) is reached. When the country is brought into contact with the world economy, the production combination moves from A to B, reflecting the fact that it has a comparative advantage in manufactured goods. The international price ratio of the two goods is given, represented by the straight line passing through B and C. Adjusting to this new price ratio, the country now produces only manufactured goods, and exports BC_2 units of manufactured goods and imports OC_1 units of primary goods. The country consumes OC_2 units of manufactured goods and OC_1 units of primary goods and enjoys the U_2 standard of living. The difference between U_2 and U_1 is a gain from international trade.

If it is argued that this depicts gains from trade accruing to Japan, a number of objections might be raised. In an actual situation, numerous products are traded; to compress them into only two goods is unrealistic. Since Japan is a net importer of primary goods and a net exporter of manufactured goods, however, the two-commodity classification represents the net balance. Another objection might be that since some imported goods cannot be produced in Japan, it is necessary to treat them separately. Cotton, oil and coffee, for example, are not produced in Japan. Yet, this does not mean that they cannot be produced there.[8] Thus, it is not absolutely necessary to treat separately the imported goods which are not produced in Japan.

Finally, the objection might be raised that the difference between U_1 and U_2 cannot be measured, so that it is impossible to know the actual magnitude of the difference. Yet, it is possible to get some feeling of the magnitude by determining the proportional increase of inputs needed to move from A to C in Figure 2. At this point, it is important to note that the gain from trade is not the ratio of trade to GNP. Today, the ratio of export/import to GNP in Japan is about 10 per cent but this does not mean that, if trade were to stop, GNP would decline by 10 per cent. In Figure 2, the ratio of export to GNP is BC_2 divided by OB, but the gain from trade is the difference between U_2 and U_1, which can be quite large. If trade were to stop now in Japan, part of the productive resources would have to be moved back to primary production, a large part of industrial production would collapse, and the standard of living would decline. Although the exact magnitude of the trade gain is not known, there is no doubt that it is substantial.

If the economy were to adjust to the international price ratio, a short-term gain would be reaped, but in the course of Japanese economic development, it appears that trade gains accrued over the long term. In the Meiji era, specialization in silk and other goods in which Japan had a comparative advantage was handicapped by the existence of a large subsistence sector. The re-allocation of resources to such goods seems to have taken place over a number of years as the money economy was further extended and the subsistence sector shrank due to improvements in transport and communications. In the post-war period, the reallocation of resources away from primary production was likewise gradual, proceeding as the government lifted barriers on the import of primary products. One important step in this direction was the government decision in the late 1950s to liberalize the import of oil and to phase out coal production which had hitherto occupied an important position in the Japanese industrial strategy.[9]

Given the degree of specialization, the terms of trade represented by the slope of the price line in Figure 2 are important in influencing the size of the gain from trade. In Figure 2, if the slope is steeper (i.e., the terms of trade more favourable), the gain is larger. If it is flatter (or the terms of trade less favourable), the gain is smaller. When discussing the gain from trade, therefore, it is important to investigate whether the terms of trade became favourable or unfavourable over the course of economic development.

G. Myrdal and R. Prebisch once argued that, with economic growth, the terms of trade[10] deteriorate for primary producers, widening the gap between developed and developing countries.[11] If this is correct, then Japan (which has been a net importer of primary products) should have gained from trade. There is, however, no empirical evidence for this contention. As shown in Table 3, there were periods in which the terms of trade improved: from the mid-1870s to the early 1900s they improved by about 30 per cent and from the late 1940s to the early 1960s by about 20 per cent. These gains were offset by the unfavourable trend from the early 1900s to the mid-1930s, and in fact, over the period of a century from the early 1870s to the early 1970s, the trend was slightly unfavourable to Japan.

The increase of the living standard from U_1 to U_2 in Figure 2 is a one-time gain, but when part of the gain is saved, it has dynamic implications. Behind the production possibility curve in Figure 2, it is assumed that the quantity of inputs is fixed, but if part of the income gain is saved, capital accumulation takes place, and the production possibility curve is pushed outward. This creates a new trade gain in the next period.

The dynamic effects of trade are not confined to this capital accumulation effect. The production possibility curve can also be pushed outward by the indirect effects of trade.[12] The first indirect effect occurs when trade improves efficiency by fostering healthy competition and keeping in check potentially inefficient oligopolies. It is well known that most manufacturing industries in Japan today are oligopolies. In fact, it is difficult to suggest an example of an industry in Japan in which many firms compete. Examples of oligopolies, on the other hand, come readily to mind: the automobile industry, steel, shipbuilding, colour television, aluminium, etc., are all oligopolies. Because of lack of domestic competition, oligopolies are considered inefficient, but when they are subject to international competition, many of the causes of inefficiency are removed. One might even argue that under free trade, oligopolies are more conducive to technological innovations, and that they therefore improve efficiency. It is quite conceivable that, because of the competition Japanese oligopolies faced in both the export and domestic markets, they were more receptive to new opportunities for technological advances which would reduce production costs.

Trade also contributes to technological progress by making it possible to import machinery and equipment which incorporate the most recent technology. In the early phase of industrialization, import of textile machinery from Britain made it possible for Japan to catch up with advanced technology, and subsequently, to outstrip British exports in the Asian market. Later, precision machinery, chemical machinery, electronic products (such as semiconductors and computers) and many other new products were imported, and the level of Japanese technology was further advanced.

The importation of machinery and equipment is not the only way to introduce technical knowledge from abroad. So-called 'dis-embodied' knowledge [that knowledge (e.g. management techniques, etc.) which is not incorporated in any particular product, usually machines] was transferred from Western countries to Japan through international contact. Large numbers of Japanese have studied in the West. Rapid development of air transportation has made it possible for Japanese corporate executives to travel abroad frequently to assess directly new investment or technological opportunities. The information network of Japanese trading companies (and, to a certain extent, banks) which was formed by linking overseas branches by telex, has made the most recent information accessible without delay. Patented knowledge had to be bought, but it was usually profitable to the recipient companies, since in some cases, the fee was very low. The fee charged by the Bell Laboratories for the patent of the transistor, for example, was only a few hundred dollars. By using this knowledge, Sony succeeded in making transistor radios and becoming perhaps the most successful company in electronics. In many cases, however, the fees were substantial [for example, synthetic fibre (nylon and polyester) technology imported in the early 1950s]. Even here, however, costs were outweighed by the gains which arose from the tremendous growth of production and export of synthetic fibres in the following years.

Another indirect effect of trade is psychological. Slightly more than a century ago, J. S. Mill wrote:

> A people (at an early stage of industrial advancement) may be in a quiescent, indolent, uncultivated state, with all their tastes either fully satisfied or entirely undeveloped, and they may fail to put forth the whole of their productive energies for want of any sufficient object of desire. The opening of a foreign trade, by making them acquainted with new objects, or tempting them by the easier acquisition of things which they had not previously thought attainable, sometimes works a sort of industrial revolution in a country whose resources were previously undeveloped for want of energy and ambition in the people: inducing those who were satisfied with scanty comforts and little work to work harder for the gratification of their new tastes, and even to save, and accumulate capital, for the still more complete satisfaction of those tastes at a future time.[13]

In modern terms, Mill is discussing here the revolution of rising expectation: that is, when a backward people meets an advanced people, the former pushes for rapid development in order to improve its miserable life. In a way, this notion reflects the feeling of an observer from an advanced country, as to how he would react if he had to live the miserable life of a backward people. If a backward people does not respond at all, the notion of the revolution of rising expectation is a mere fantasy. In view of the importance of material motives in human behaviour, however, a complete absence of response is unlikely. The response may not be revolutionary, but it does take place. Japan, through contact with the West, came to know of high Western standards of living, and was greatly stimulated to achieve something similar. Otherwise, it is difficult to understand the presence in contemporary Japan of many goods and services (e.g., colour television, cars, stereophonic equipment, golf, etc.) which originated in the West. Mill may have exaggerated the speed of response, but he was essentially right at least in claiming that the contact with an advanced nation stimulates economic development.

The puzzling question, if trade made such a large contribution to Japanese economic development, why did it not do the same for other developing countries, remains.[14] Most developing countries that were brought into contact with the world market, experienced a steady rise in exports. Yet the export sector did not become the propelling force for economic development as it did in Japan.

One possible explanation is that developing countries export primary products whose linkage effects tend to be weak. Japan, on the other hand, exported manufactured goods whose production bestows a variety of benefits through linkage effects and the training of human skill. This argument, however, ignores the fact that Japan exported primary products (tea and silk) in the early phase of development.[15]

As a counter-argument, one might insist that silk has greater linkage effects than most of the primary products developing countries export today, but this is difficult to accept as the major explanation for the different economic performances between Japan and developing countries. As an illustration of this point, contrast Japan with Brazil. The forward linkages of coffee (a major product in Brazil) are weak, since all that needs to be done for the coffee beans is to grind them. The forward linkage effects of silk are greater, since raw silk goes through reeling, weaving and needlework before it reaches the consumer. If the backward linkage is considered, however, the opposite conclusions are drawn: coffee requires fertilizer, whereas the basic input of the production of raw silk is the leaves of mulberry trees. Mulberry trees require some fertilizer, but there was little use of chemical fertilizer, and thus, in the Meiji era, its linkage effect on the chemical industry was almost nil. Hence, after both forward and backward linkages are considered, it is not entirely clear which commodities have more beneficial effects on economic development.

At such points as this, it is tempting to think of the state as a *deus ex machina*. Nevertheless, it still seems possible to characterize past government in Brazil as an élitist government. For many years, owners of coffee plantations (who came originally from Portugal and other parts of Europe) controlled the Brazilian government and did little for the rest of the population (mostly blacks brought from Africa to be plantation workers). In contrast, the Japanese power élite was more dedicated to the national cause and more eager to break down class barriers. To them, economic development was necessarily a socially integrated process. This ideal is reflected, for example, in the system of universal compulsory education initiated several years after the Meiji Restoration. In Brazil, the masses were left uneducated, and as a consequence, human capital formation was seriously retarded.

If developing states are dedicated to national development, as Japan was, and if they use wisely the tax revenue from export proceeds, the effect of export growth on economic development can be more favourable. It is also important that a link between the export industry and the traditional sector be established. In many developing countries, since there had been no response by domestic entrepreneurs (or, more likely, a lack of technical competence on their part in matters of international trade) foreign capital came in, and an export industry was established. This industry remains an 'enclave' since the rest of the economy cannot or will not respond to new opportunities made available by trade. This dualism is more a reflection of underdevelopment than its cause.

In Japan, there has been a different kind of dualism, between the modern sector (in which production technique is capital intensive) and the traditional sector (in which small enterprises are dominant and production techniques labour intensive). In the Japanese dualism, however, the traditional sector has been the major exporter for many years, and has supported the growth of the modern sector. Silk, fabrics, garments, toys and plastics—the products of the traditional sector—were important foreign exchange earners until the early 1960s when heavy industrial goods began to play a central role in Japanese exports. From the beginning of the modern period, as a result of commercialization in the Tokugawa period, there was a response by domestic entrepreneurs to the new profit opportunities created by trade, and this export sector was linked to the rest of the economy through the market institution. Although this linkage was somewhat weak in the early modern period, it became more firmly established as the money economy was further extended, and it reduced the size of the subsistence sector during the course of development. In Japan there was no such sharp division as exists in many developing countries between the export industry and the rest of the economy in the level of skill, the availability of capital, or the quality of entrepreneurship.

1. Important among political factors were the anti-foreign sentiments harboured by many discontented samurai which sometimes resulted in terrorist attacks on Japanese merchants engaged in foreign trade, and the shogunate's interference in export activities.

2. The factor proportion is the ratio of one factor of production to another. In this context, it is the ratio of capital to labour.

3. Akamatsu Kaname discusses international trade from the viewpoint of complementarity and substitution. See *Sekai Keizai Ron* [Discourse on the world economy], Tokyo, Kunimoto Shobo, 1965, Chapter 7.

4. For a more detailed discussion on the three trade models, consult a standard textbook on international trade, such as R. Jones and R. Caves, *World Trade and Payments: An Introduction*, Boston, Little, Brown and Co., 1973.

5. Kanamori Hisao, *Nihon no Boeki* [Japanese trade], Tokyo, Shiseido, 1961, pp. 145–6.

6. I. B. Kravis, 'Trade as a Handmaiden of Growth: Similarities between the Nineteenth and Twentieth Centuries', *Economic Journal*, December 1970; and H. G. Johnson, *Economic Policies Toward Less Developed Countries*, Washington, The Brookings Institution, 1967, p. 65.

7. Denis Robertson, *Essays in Monetary Theory*, St. Albans, Staples Press, 1948, p. 214.

8. During the Tokugawa period, cotton was grown in Japan. Also, some oil is produced today, although the quantity produced domestically is miniscule compared with the quantity consumed. In this case, it may be better to consider that oil can be replaced with coal, with which Japan is more favourably endowed. Coffee can be grown in a greenhouse if necessary, or tea can be considered a substitute.

9. This relatively early switch from coal to oil was an important factor for rapid economic growth in the 1960s and the early 1970s. Contrast this with the British case, where the switch could not be made easily because of the existence of a powerful trade union of coal mine workers.

10. The terms of trade is defined as the ratio of export prices to import prices.

11. R. Prebisch, *Towards a New Trade Policy for Development*, United Nations, 1964, and G. Myrdal, *International Economy*, New York, Harper and Row, 1956.

12. The indirect effects of trade were first discussed by J. S. Mill. See *Principles of Political Economy*, London, Longman, Green and Co., 1923, Book III, Chapter XVII.

13. Ibid., p. 481.

14. A good summary of why trade did not lead to development in other countries is given in G. Meier, *Leading Issues in Economic Development* (third edition), London, Oxford University Press, 1976, pp. 717–23.

15. As explained earlier, silk is here considered a primary product since it was produced by farm households.

IV

Preparedness for Modernization

IF JAPAN HAD BECOME A COLONY

TO most Western observers who arrived in mid-nineteenth century Asia, Japan appeared to be as backward as any other Asian country. Yet, in the next half century, Japan alone among them emerged as a modern state. What was it that set Japan apart from the other Asian countries? This chapter looks at the Japan of the 1850s, and contrasts its preparedness for modernization with that of other Asian countries.

It is sometimes argued that Japan's success at modernization was due solely to the fact that Japan had not been colonized by Western Powers, as had other Asian countries. Contrasting Japan with India, Paul Baran, a Marxist economist, contends that Japan developed because it was independent, while India remained backward because of exploitation by the British during the colonial period.[1] Clifford Geertz, an anthropologist, claims that Japan was similar to Java in many respects in the mid-nineteenth century: both were heavily populated, both were engaged in labour intensive rice cultivation and both had roughly the same rice yield per hectare. In attempting to account for the difference in economic performance between the two countries in the following century, Geertz suggests that agricultural surpluses in Java were siphoned off to the mother country, the Netherlands, and were not used, as in Japan, for capital accumulation and technological progress.[2]

But why was Japan not colonized in the mid-nineteenth century? Baran's answer is that Japan was simply lucky. It was poor in resources and not attractive as a market, so that Western Powers were not terribly interested in the country. Moreover, Britain, the major imperial power at that time, was busy elsewhere, and could not devote much of its attention to Japan. Other Western Powers, France in particular, were looking for opportunities to establish colonies in Asia, but rivalry among them worked favourably for Japan. In short, according to Baran, the fact that Japan was not colonized was an accident of history.

Was Japan really such a potentially easy prey for the Western Powers as Baran claims? Unlike South and South-East Asian countries which were readily colonized, Japan had experienced several centuries of cultural unification and the spread of a national ideology that made the Japanese well aware of their cultural identity and suspicious of any foreign intrusion. Also, the ability of Japanese leaders to discern the implications of the arrival of Western emissaries and to carry out appropriate reforms was unparalleled in other Asian countries.

This is not to suggest that there was no element of luck involved in Japan's transition to a modern nation, but in the 1850s, when Perry forced open Japan's doors, the historical setting in no way suggested that Japan would emerge a few decades later as a modern state. Various possible scenarios can be conceived for this period. For example, if the last Tokugawa shogun had accepted the offer of help from the French and decided to meet the military challenge of the opposition to the end, part of Japan might have become colonized. Or, if many provincial lords had decided to keep their fiefs instead of surrendering them to the emperor in the early Meiji era, large-scale civil war might have ensued, and Japan's modernization might have been considerably delayed. Clearly, there were elements of 'luck' in Japan's modernization, but for reasons different from those Baran suggests.

It is always tempting to blame colonial policy for the underdevelopment of South and South-East Asia, but before this view is fully accepted, it is necessary to question the extent to which political independence is a guarantee of economic development. A comparison between Thailand and Burma is both useful in this regard and appropriate. Both countries have the same religion, race and climate, and are similar in many other respects. According to the view that political independence promotes economic development while colonialism suppresses it, Thailand should be ahead of Burma in the level of economic development, since Thailand was spared the colonial experience, while Burma suffered long (from the 1870s to the 1940s) as a British colony. Both, however, are underdeveloped countries today. The difference in their political histories has not made much difference in their economic performances. This seems to suggest that there are other factors besides political independence involved in economic development.

CONTRAST WITH THAILAND

Since political independence does not seem to be the sole factor in economic development, what other factors might have existed to differentiate Japan from a country like Thailand, which appears similar in so many respects? First, the difference cannot be said to be due to the tardiness of attempts at modernization in Thailand. King Chulalongkorn (1868–1910) who ruled Thailand during roughly the same time as the Meiji era, was also convinced of the need to modernize. He undertook a number of institutional reforms (including the emancipation of slaves, establishment of a secular educational system, construction of railways, institution of a postal service, reform of the laws and the court system, and creation of a public health service) and his reign is widely regarded as one of the greatest in Thai dynastic history.

Thai attempts at modernization did not stop with the death of King Chulalongkorn. With renewed vigour, Field

Marshall Pibul Songkram, who became Prime Minister of Thailand twice during the period 1938–57, undertook a number of measures to inspire nationalistic spirit among the Thai people and to push economic development under state initiative. Every Prime Minister after him has been likewise committed to economic development.

That Thailand has remained underdeveloped does not mean that no changes have occurred within the country. Multi-storeyed, air-conditioned hotels and airports, telephones, highways, cars, various export crops and the other evidence of modernity did not, obviously, exist at the beginning of King Chulalongkorn's reign. However, these quantitative changes have not brought about a qualitative change in the life of most of the Thai population.[3] The present symbols of modernity serve only a small segment of the population, while the bulk of the people remain uneducated and poverty-stricken, a situation in sharp contrast with Japan.

Some anthropologists argue that the reasons for Thailand's failure to modernize lie in the social structure of the country. When they visit Thailand, such observers are often struck by the easy-going character of the Thai people. Group discipline is weak; there is no strong sense of obligation and duty to others; there is no intense insular patriotism; and a closely woven pattern of co-operation in agricultural work is lacking. In short, Thai behaviour is highly individualistic, and Thai society is, as John Embree, an American anthropologist, has termed it, a 'loosely structured society'.[4]

Japanese society is completely the opposite. In the mid-nineteenth century, the Japanese value system centred around personal obligation. In the early Tokugawa period, obligation was a personal or internal value which demanded that the recipient of a favour return that favour and prove himself worthy of trust. As social stratification progressed, however, obligation came increasingly to be defined in terms of external social obligation, taking the form of obligation to one's lord (loyalty), to parents (filial piety), to friends and neighbours, and to the community.[5] These obligations had to be fulfilled in order for one to be accepted as a member of society. If one were to refuse or neglect them, the inevitable consequence was social ostracism. The concept of shame in the 'culture of shame', as Ruth Benedict characterized Japanese culture,[6] can be interpreted as the fear of failure to fulfil obligation. To the extent that this fear is the norm of behaviour, Japanese culture can be considered to be a culture of shame. In a society where obligation occupies such an important position, group discipline is strong and individual behaviour is highly constrained. John Embree considered this to be the main characteristic of Japanese society, calling it a tightly knit society.[7]

THE TOKUGAWA HERITAGE

Japan's level of income in the mid-nineteenth century, before modernization began, was close to subsistence (see Table 2), and in this sense, Japan was as backward as Thailand and other Asian countries.[8] However, in the capacity for internal change and for economic development, Japan must be differentiated from these countries. This is perhaps a result of the tightly knit social structure previously discussed and other heritages of the Tokugawa period. Among important developments of the pre-modern period, one may cite, for example, growth in education, political development and commercialization.

TOKUGAWA EDUCATION

Late Tokugawa Japan was a highly literate society, as may be seen in the following description of the literary culture in the late Tokugawa period.

It [Japan in the late Tokugawa period] was a world in which books abounded. Their production gave employment to several thousands of persons in the official school presses and in the free enterprise publishing houses which sold their wares to the public. Works of scholarship now accounted for only a small part of the total output. There were story books, pornographic books, travel guides, novels, poems, collections of sermons; and they were bought, or borrowed at so much a day from book peddlers, not simply by the samurai, but also, or even chiefly, by members of the other classes.[9]

This situation may be contrasted with that in Thailand where it was not until 1828 that the first printing press for the Thai language was set up (and even then it was established by a foreigner, and in Singapore). In 1873, a printing press was set up in Thailand, but it was used exclusively for printing missionary books.[10] Thai society in the mid-nineteenth century was far from being 'a world in which books abounded'.

The content as well as the level of education in the late Tokugawa period had an important bearing on the speed at which Japan absorbed Western science and technology after the Meiji Restoration. The various sects of Buddhism, which had dominated the intellectual life of Japan for the millenium before the Tokugawa period, lost their influence over Japanese intellectuals. In the early seventeenth century, Neo-Confucianism replaced it as the major doctrine and provided the philosophical basis for a this-worldly orientation. Because of its heavy emphasis on self-cultivation as the basic solution to social problems, however, Neo-Confucianism came under attack towards the end of the century by another school of Confucianism, and subsequently lost its dominant position in scholarship.

As the criticism of Neo-Confucianism mounted (around 1700) the school of thought called 'Practical Learning', which included the study of agriculture, surveying, mathematics, medicine, astronomy and natural history, freed itself from Neo-Confucian influence, to the extent that utility or usefulness became the guiding principle. The next important turning point in intellectual history came in the early eighteenth century when the study of Western science—called 'Dutch Learning'—was given official approval. In the following years, as Dutch Learning proved its usefulness, the Practical Learning school also became more firmly established as a respectable branch of scholarship. Because of these past advances, therefore, when Japan began to modernize in the mid-nineteenth century, Western science and technology were not unknown to Japanese intellectuals.

The intellectual climate was quite different in the mid-nineteenth century in Thailand. The centres of education were the Buddhist temples, and mysticism was central to their teachings. When cholera spread across the country, it was a common Thai practice then to resort to magical ritual to propitiate the gods.[11] Undoubtedly, magic played a large part in the popular imagination of Tokugawa Japan, but there was a large intellectual élite with a far more rational view of the world.

TOKUGAWA BUREAUCRACY

Westerners who came to Japan in the mid-nineteenth century apparently had difficulty in determining precisely who was the ruler of the country. Was he the emperor at Kyoto or the shogun at Edo? In Tokugawa Japan, the emperor was the ruler in theory, but in practice, his was a nominal rule in which he conferred the authority to govern the country on the shogun. The shogun, similarly, did not rule the country directly. His fiefs extended through various parts of the country (comprising about one-fourth of the land), but the rest was divided into about 270 domains called *han* and ruled by his vassals, the daimyo. The ultimate authority to rule the domain resided in the shogun, but he rarely interfered in the internal affairs of the domain. In a sense, Tokugawa Japan consisted of some 270 autonomous states. In matters of security, coinage, foreign policy, and other national and inter-domain affairs, however, the shogun exerted his authority. Also, in order to keep daimyo under control, a 'hostage' system was instituted, under which daimyo were required to live in Edo in alternate years.

In the domains, as in the shogun's government, elaborate administrative systems were established. Marxist historians often quote the brutal remark attributed to the founder of the Tokugawa dynasty, Tokugawa Ieyasu, to the effect that peasants should be treated so that they would 'neither live nor die', and thus tend to characterize the Tokugawa administrative system as highly exploitative. To what extent Ieyasu's thought was put into practice is debatable, but without question the administrative machinery was pervasive and efficient enough to extract from peasants tribute amounting to as much as 50 per cent of their crop. One strength of the system lay in the ability to buy off wealthy peasants and to impose group responsibility on villages, but it was also important that the rulers be members of the warrior class who could use military force against anyone who questioned their authority. The submissive attitude of the Japanese in the modern period is closely linked with the supremacy of the warrior class established in the pre-modern period.

The effectiveness of the Tokugawa bureaucracy is well demonstrated by the fact that it managed to govern a population of over 30 million for a period of approximately 250 years with little evidence of political breakdown. Undoubtedly, the authoritarian nature of government was the most important factor in this political stability, but it should be noted at the same time that developments within the bureaucracy also made important contributions. In the area of functional differentiation, for example, after the mid-seventeenth century when peace was firmly established, the bureaucracy became predominantly a civil administration. As the civil bureaucracy became increasingly important, there was also an increase in the educational level of the samurai. Samurai at the end of the Tokugawa period, unlike their early seventeenth century predecessors, who placed primary emphasis on martial arts at the expense of reading and writing, were literate and had knowledge of history, philosophy and politics. As the educational level of the samurai increased, government became more impersonal and legally defined.[12]

Yet, there were many problems in the Tokugawa bureaucracy. For one, there came to be an over-abundance of samurai for the work required. For another, because of the importance attached to status, the application of the concept of meritocracy was limited and thus, the Tokugawa bureaucracy could not be passed on *in toto* to the modern period. Nevertheless, it must be acknowledged that the effectiveness of the Meiji bureaucracy owed a great deal to what it inherited from the Tokugawa period: the administrative expertise of the samurai constituted the backbone of the Meiji administration; the Tokugawa village administration was retained in its entirety; and domain administration provided a basis for the establishment of modern local administration. Without these legacies from the Tokugawa period, it would have been extremely difficult to carry out appropriate reforms and to maintain political discipline in the critical period of transition to a modern nation.

COMMERCIALIZATION

According to the German historical school of the nineteenth century there are three stages of development from the point of view of the methods of exchange.[13] In the first stage, goods are exchanged for other goods. In the second stage, money is used as a means of payment in transactions. In the final stage, transactions are based on credit. The economy in the first stage is called a natural economy, that in the second stage a money economy, and that in the third stage a credit economy. Under this scheme of classification, the early Middle Ages of Europe (ninth to twelfth centuries) is considered a period of natural economy. This characterization is, however, wrong if we consider the term natural economy to mean an economy without money, for money did exist at that time. Nevertheless, since the man-

or (the basic economic structure of that time), was largely self-sufficient, the role played by money in the economy was very limited.

The Tokugawa economy was a feudal one which shared several features with the early medieval economy of Europe and it is tempting to characterize it as a natural economy. A close look at the Tokugawa economy reveals, however, that exchanges involving money and credit were more than negligible. In this period, the major type of money was coins minted by the Tokugawa shogunate. Provincial governments also issued paper money for circulation within the domain, largely to raise additional revenue. In major cities, credit instruments backed by established exchange brokers circulated as private money. How much money was in circulation in this period is not known exactly, but that it was not a negligible amount can be seen from the following data on coins. In 1869 (the second year of the Meiji era), approximately 87.9 million yen equivalent of gold coins were in circulation, 52.7 million yen equivalent of silver coins, and 6.0 million yen equivalent of subsidiary coins.[14]

The use of credit was also widespread, especially in major cities. According to an Osaka merchant at the end of the Tokugawa period, almost 99 per cent of all transactions among Osaka merchants used credit instruments, and cash payment was rare. This may be an exaggeration, but the use of credit instruments was undoubtedly commonplace among Osaka merchants. In other major cities, the use of credit may have been slightly more limited, but credit exchanges were undoubtedly a familiar practice.[15]

The economic philosophy of the Tokugawa bureaucracy placed emphasis on agriculture as the major source of wealth and the peasants engaged in this industry were given the highest theoretical status among commoners. In contrast, commerce was considered unproductive and merchants supposedly occupied the lowest social position in the Tokugawa pecking order. Ironically, however, over the years commerce increased in importance in the economic life of the period and merchants became enormously influential. The rise of commerce may not be surprising to those familiar with the increased importance of commercial transactions in the late Middle Ages in Western Europe. In a way, it might be argued that the natural economy of feudalism was bound to give way to a money economy sooner or later.

In the context of Tokugawa Japan, the rise of a money economy was conditioned by two things in particular. First, all samurai were required to live in castle towns (the headquarters of provincial administration). Removed from agriculture, they became rentiers and needed the help of merchants to exchange part of their rice stipends for daily necessities. Another important contribution to commercial development was the hostage system, mentioned previously. Because this system required daimyo to travel between their domains and Edo, and to live at Edo in alternate years, it contributed to the development of interprovincial transactions. Rice and other commodities in demand outside domains had to be raised and sold for hard currency, which could be used to finance the necessities arising from the system. Development of coastal shipping, post towns and financial and commercial institutions owed a great deal to this system.

The rise of commerce shook the foundations of Tokugawa feudalism and was a contributing factor to the Meiji Restoration. Yet, since merchants were closely tied to feudal interests, they had no strong desire to destroy the existing system in favour of a new one. As will be explained in the following chapter, the Meiji Restoration was not a bourgeois revolution. Rather, the significance of Tokugawa commerce lies in the commercial and financial institutions which developed in this period and which facilitated industrialization and economic development in the subsequent period. The German historical school referred to above may not be entirely correct in its scheme of classification, but the point that a modern economy cannot exist without money and credit remains valid. A natural economy cannot be the basis for economic development.

CONTRAST WITH CHINA

When Japan's preparation for modernization in the mid-nineteenth century is compared with that in China, the distinctions are not as clear cut as in the case of South and South-East Asian countries. In fact, if a Western observer arriving in East Asia in the mid-nineteenth century were asked which country would have a better chance of meeting the Western challenge, most probably would have bet on China. China was better prepared, psychologically, for dealing with foreigners. While the Japanese were insular and inexperienced in foreign dealings after two centuries of seclusion, the Chinese were urbane and self-confident. In terms of social structure, also, it appeared that there was more dynamism in the Chinese system. Chinese society was less stratified, the merchant class had a wider scope of freedom, and the high civil bureaucracy was recruited on a merit basis. Also, the natural resource endowment and size of the country served to give China an advantage. Japan, on the other hand, was a small country, overpopulated and possessed few natural resources.[16]

Yet, Japan fared better than China in meeting the Western challenge. While China was forced to give territorial concessions and commercial privileges to the Western Powers (becoming a 'hyper-colony'—exploited by all but the responsibility of none), Japan first protected itself from the Western intrusion, and then went on to renegotiate the unequal treaties it had been forced to accept at the end of the Tokugawa period. In the Sino-Japanese War (1894–5), Japan demonstrated a clear military superiority over China. Then, in the Russo-Japanese War (1904–5), Japan defeated Russia and joined the league of imperial powers. In the following years, China became the major victim of Japanese imperialism. In the field of economics as well, Japan's performance was more impressive and this is reflected in the present level of development. While China remains an underdeveloped country, Japan is an industrial nation enjoying a much higher standard of living.

One factor favouring Japan in meeting the Western challenge was that it was historically a cultural borrower. From the early centuries of the Christian era, China was a source of knowledge, particularly through the institution of Chinese Buddhism and Confucianism. It can be argued that for such a cultural borrower, there were fewer psychological inhibitions toward adopting Western technology when its superiority was clearly demonstrated. By the mid-nineteenth century the assimilation process was so complete that Japan had a unique culture which acted as an inner source of pride, counterbalancing whatever inferiority complex might have accompanied heavy borrowing from those who had hitherto been regarded as 'hairy barbarians'. The phrase 'Western Science and Oriental Morality', which meant that the West excelled in science but was inferior to the Orient (Japan in particular) in culture, gave a sense of pride to the Japanese who might otherwise have lost their cultural identification in the swirling process of modernization.

Differences in the political systems of China and Japan also had bearing on the pattern of their responses to the Western challenge. In China, political power was centralized and the chief local administrators were appointed by the central government. Japan, however, was divided into some 270 provinces, each of which had virtual autonomy, and usually, the head of a province (daimyo) was the hereditary heir from within the same family. When Japan faced the Western challenge, its political stability was disturbed and the legitimacy of the shogunate was seriously questioned. In this period of political change, the Tokugawa system made it easier for those provinces which opposed the shogunate to emerge as a counterforce and establish a new regime.[17] Since under some circumstances political power can be more effective when centralized than when divided, there was some theoretical advantage in the Chinese system; but the confrontation with the West came at an inopportune time during the declining phase of the then ruling Ch'ing dynasty. It seems that, in general, when political power is centralized and corrupt, a much longer time is required to destroy the ancient regime and to set up a new one than when political power is divided. The decentralized Japanese system was not, however, free from trouble; there was the danger that prolonged civil war might ensue and the country be split. The existence of the emperor, a common history and a common culture, however, exerted a centripetal force which counteracted the forces which broke apart the shogunate by providing a rallying point for otherwise dissident elements. Thus, it is more accurate to argue that the combination of these factors with political decentralization actually facilitated Japan's transition to the modern period.

The quality of leadership of the two countries should also be considered. It is sometimes argued that the fact that 'foreigners' ruled China delayed its modernization. The Ch'ing dynasty was a Manchu dynasty, and the Manchus were at first regarded as foreigners. They had their own language, and initially, stood apart culturally from the Chinese, but the Manchu leaders were soon assimilated into Chinese culture during the course of their rule in China. Those who blame the Ch'ing dynasty for China's delay in modernization question whether its leaders were really dedicated to national interest, by quoting the remark attributed to Prince Ch'un, the representative of the Empress Dowager, that 'it were better to hand over the Empire to the Foreign Devils, than to surrender it to the dictation of these Chinese rebels'.[18] It is unlikely that Ch'ing dynasty leaders completely disregarded China's interests, but in view of the way in which the leaders dealt with the Western Powers, they can be rightly accused of being interested primarily in maintaining their own rule, even at the expense of national integrity.

Their attitude can be contrasted with the intense nationalism of Japanese leaders in the mid-nineteenth century. According to the political ideology which had been rapidly gaining influence among the samurai at that time, Japan was a divine country which must not be contaminated by 'hairy barbarians' from other countries; to rule the country well and protect it from those barbarians were the primary obligations of the ruling class. The education and martial arts of the samurai were considered important, not of themselves, but for the purpose of fulfilling such obligations. This ideology set in motion political changes when the Western Powers arrived in Japan in the 1850s.

After witnessing the defeat of China in the Opium War of 1840, and observing at first hand the superiority of Western weapons in Japan, the Tokugawa shogunate accepted the demands of the Western Powers to open the country. This was probably unavoidable in view of the gap in military strength between the West and Japan, but it was considered by those who subscribed to the chauvinistic political ideology to be an indication of failure to govern the country well; it thus gave legitimacy to the movement to overthrow the shogunate. This movement resulted in the Meiji Restoration in 1868. In the meantime, as the movement's leaders came into closer contact with some Western Powers and learned of their clear military superiority, they too gave up thoughts of expelling the 'Western Barbarians' and began to feel it necessary to open the country and learn Western technology.[19] The chauvinistic nationalism did not, however, completely disappear; it remained in the form of dedication to national honour and glory, and was a propelling force during the Meiji modernization.

1. P. Baran, *The Political Economy of Growth*, New York, Monthly Review Press, 1957, pp. 151–61.

2. C. Geertz, *Agricultural Involution*, Berkeley, University of California Press, 1963, pp. 130–54.

3. If one makes an analogy to an aeroplane, the point may be made as follows: economic changes in the past have moved the plane along the ground, but the stage of 'take-off' has not been reached since the plane has not, so to speak, achieved a 'critical ground speed'.

4. J. Embree, 'Thailand–A Loosely Structured Social System', in H. Evers (ed.), *Loosely Structured Social Systems: Thailand in Comparative Perspective*, Southeast Asian Studies, Yale University, 1969.

5. Minamoto Ryoen, *Giri to Ninjo* ['Giri' and 'ninjo'], Tokyo, Chuo Koron Sha, 1969, pp. 59–67.

6. R. Benedict, *The Chrysanthemum and the Sword*, Boston, Houghton Mifflin Co., 1946.

7. Embree, op. cit., p. 12.

8. E. H. Norman, a Canadian historian of Japan, wrote:

> The modern observer of the Far East is apt to forget that in the middle of the 19th century Japan was as weak as contemporary Burma or Siam (Thailand), . . . with no monies in its treasury, its industry still handicraft, its trade negligible, its poverty profound, . . . This was the Japan which the Meiji Government inherited.

J. Dower (ed.), *Origins of the Modern Japanese State: Selected Writings of E. H. Norman*, New York, Pantheon Books, 1975, p. 153.

9. R. Dore, *Tokugawa Education*, Berkeley, University of California Press, 1965, p. 2.

10. Prasert Chittiwatanapong, 'The Modernization Base in Japan and Thailand: Education and Science', in *The Emergence of Modern States: Thailand and Japan*, Thailand–Japan Studies Program, 1976, p. 18.

11. Prasert Chittiwatanapong, ibid., p. 18.

12. For a more detailed discussion on the Tokugawa bureaucracy, see J. Hall, 'The Nature of Traditional Society: Japan', in R. Ward and D. Rustow (eds.), *Political Modernization in Japan and Turkey*, Princeton, Princeton University Press, 1964.

13. For further discussion on this point, see M. Postan, 'The Rise of a Money Economy', *Economic History Review*, 1944, No. 2.

14. Sakudo Yotaro, 'The Reform of the Monetary System in the Early Years of Meiji', *Osaka Economic Papers*, September 1957, pp. 33–4. One yen was roughly equivalent to US$1 at that time.

15. This discussion of credit is summarized from general histories

of the period in Japanese. See, for example, Sakudo Yotaro, *Kinsei Nihon Kahei Shi* [History of money in early modern Japan], Tokyo, Kobundo, 1958.

16. For China's advantage over Japan, see W. Lockwood, 'Japan's Response to the West–the Contrast with China', *World Politics*, October 1965, pp. 41–2.

17. W. Lockwood discusses this from the viewpoint of creative tension. See ibid.

18. Quoted in J. Dower (ed.), *Origins of the Modern Japanese State: Selected Writings of E. H. Norman*, New York, Pantheon Books, 1975, p. 231.

19. How the content of the ideology which legitimated the Restoration movement changed over time is discussed in Sakata Yoshio 'Nihon Kindaika no Shuppatsu to Tenkai' [The 'Take Off' and Expansion of Japan's Modernization], *The Jinbun Gakuho*, March 1970. In this article, Sakata also points out that the fact that the intelligentsia were the samurai (warriors) in Japan whereas they were the literati in China accounts for the different responses to the Western challenge in the subsequent years.

V

Institutional Reforms

MEIJI REFORMS

The two most important events in the political history of modern Japan were the Meiji Restoration of 1868 and defeat in World War II, for they were the only events which brought about a break in leadership and major political reorganization. When such momentous political changes take place, institutions are usually altered to suit the purposes of the new regime. This was certainly the case after the Meiji Restoration and World War II. In the first case, various feudal institutions were abolished and new ones created; in the second, the military and its supporting institutions were abolished, and in their places, democratic and non-military ones established. These political developments are discussed in this chapter in order to throw some light on the interaction between politics and the economy.

In theory, the collapse of a feudal system is preceded by social and economic changes which undermine the basis of its institutions; and Japan was no exception to this rule. Despite rules and regulations aimed at petrifying the feudal structure of society, a money economy spread in the late Tokugawa period, shaking the foundation of the feudal system. As the samurai became urban dwellers, and discarded their traditional habits of frugality, government expenditures tended to increase, and consequently government budgets were chronically in deficits. At first, the deficits were met by borrowing money from merchants, but the interest incurred made the situation worse in later years. To solve the problem, the shogunate and many provincial governments modified their economic policies to maintain self-sufficiency, and encouraged the production of commercial crops and manufactures which could be sold in major cities. When these measures were not successful (as was most often the case) the stipends of the samurai were cut, to such an extent that low-ranking samurai were forced to do piecework at home in order to make ends meet. Conversely, many wealthy merchants were given permission to use surnames and to wear swords—the privileges of the samurai class—and allowed to participate in government administration. Although merchants supposedly occupied the lowest social status in Tokugawa society, their influence increased greatly in the late Tokugawa period as economic problems became increasingly more important concerns of the samurai class.

The feudal foundations were also being shaken in the village. Constant government attempts to increase rice taxes in order to reduce deficits made the lives of peasants yet more difficult: some of them rebelled, or left the villages for the cities (in defiance of regulations designed to keep them on the land). Also, the spread of commercial crops increased the importance of commercial transactions in the village economy and began to erode the basis of the natural economy—the economic basis of feudalism. The influence of commercialization on the village economy became particularly disturbing towards the end of the Tokugawa period (1860–7) when prices began to fluctuate widely as a consequence of the opening of trade with Western countries.

The spread of the money economy developed institutions alien to the feudal system and created a gap between the ideal of feudalism and the reality. Yet, the leading role in institutional change was not played by the merchant class. In this sense, the Meiji Restoration, which swept away feudal institutions and regulations, was not a bourgeois revolution, although a large part of the money required to finance the Restoration movement was obtained from merchants. Economic development also took place through institutional reforms in the early Meiji. These points, however, are not sufficient to argue (as some Japanese historians of Marxist leaning have) that the Meiji Restoration was a bourgeois revolution. For one thing, although money was borrowed from merchants, they were not, by any means, organized as a class in support of the movement; only certain merchants supported the shogunate and contributed funds to its military campaigns. Concerning institutional reforms in the Meiji, the creation of a militarily strong nation was as important a policy to the Meiji leaders as economic development. They often placed a higher priority on the military aspect of modernization and considered economic development a means to that end, but the goal of achieving a strong military was never subordinate to that of economic development. Thus, it is difficult to argue that the Restoration was carried out solely to further economic development. Even if it is granted that a strong military was necessary for economic development, the hypothesis that the Meiji Restoration was brought about by the bourgeoisie is unacceptable. If that were the case, the absence of leadership by the merchant class in the Restoration movement and the subordinate position of the bourgeoisie in the Meiji government cannot be adequately explained. Furthermore, that the leadership of the movement came from economically much less advanced western provinces such as Choshu and Satsuma (not from those in the areas around Edo and Osaka where a higher stage of commercial, industrial and financial development had been reached) becomes inexplicable.

The leading actors in the Meiji Restoration were the lower samurai of Choshu, Satsuma and a few other western provinces, and the various institutional reforms in the early Meiji era were undertaken by the progressively minded among these lower samurai. Capitalistic development which began in the Meiji era was a consequence of these reforms. In contrast to the Marxian view of the pattern of historical development (that the economic substructure changes first, followed by social and political changes), in Meiji Japan social and political changes triggered economic changes. The dictum normally attributed to former president of Ghana, Nkrumah, 'Seek ye first the political kingdom and all other things will be added unto you', seems more appropriate for understanding the process of historical change in the Meiji Restoration.[1]

Institutional reforms carried out in the first five years of the Meiji period consisted of political reform and socio-economic reform. The political reform removed the daimyo from power and established a centralized state. This was accomplished through *hanseki hokan* (return of the land registers) in 1869 and *haihan chiken* (abolition of fiefs and establishment of prefectures) in 1871. The ease of this transfer of power was surprising, considering that a large-scale political reorganization is bound to meet resistance from those adversely affected. One cannot but wonder why the daimyo so meekly accepted a reform that caused them to lose all their land and political power.

In attempting to answer this question, it must be remembered that the daimyo did not have a psychological attachment to land, as did princes and lords in some other feudal or semi-feudal societies. Since the daimyo were given land in return for loyalty to the shogun, they and their retainers owned it theoretically; the peasants who cultivated the land were presumably hired labourers or tenants. However, since the daimyo and their retainers lived in castle towns as administrators, the rice and other agricultural produce they collected increasingly became taxes rather than rent,[2] and they lost their emotional attachment to the land. Thus, there was no strong psychological barrier to parting with it.

There were economic interests in the land, certainly, and loss of land meant loss of the income from it. But, resistance based on this consideration was weak, partly because of the degree of financial difficulties most provinces experienced towards the end of the Tokugawa period. Many provinces could not foresee the possibility of paying debts and balancing their budgets in the near future. The fact that the new government guaranteed economic security to the daimyo, while removing the administrative headaches, was a successful ploy.

The daimyo were also psychologically disarmed by the manipulation of imperial symbols and the appeal to patriotism by the new government's leaders. By arguing that in order to meet the threat of Western imperialism, a new, unified political system had to be established with the emperor as head of the state, the new leaders created an atmosphere of immediacy which suggested that to resist the political reform was tantamount to treason. Also, the timing of the reform was advantageous to the new government's leaders; during the first several years after the Restoration, the nation was in a constant state of flux, and the daimyo were better prepared for political changes. In a way, the daimyo were defeated by the psychological warfare employed by the new government leaders.

This does not mean, however, that the new government underestimated the importance of a strong military in carrying out the political reform. In fact, a major objective of the government in the early Meiji period was to create a modern army recruited from all social classes and equipped with the newest weapons; indeed, the government was willing to demonstrate its strength if the daimyo were to resist the reform. The government had under its command the most powerful army in the country at that time; it would have, eventually, been able to crush the resistance of any daimyo. In such a case, however, the country would have been dragged into prolonged civil war and the subsequent course of modernization would have been adversely affected. It is significant that the new government accomplished this major political reform without using force—a rare historical event indeed.

Social and economic reforms constituted the second part of the institutional reforms carried out in the early Meiji era. The feudal Tokugawa society had been a class society, ascriptive as well as hierarchical. One major social reform in the early Meiji was to abolish the class system and to establish an achievement oriented society. In other words, the reform at least made it possible for people with talent and ability to advance in society, irrespective of their social backgrounds. In line with this, the government opened the bureaucracy and armed forces to people of all classes by introducing a merit system; it also established a universal compulsory education system to bring up new talent and provide equal opportunities for education. As a consequence of this reform, merchants and peasants became the social equals of former samurai who lost their monopoly of arms and government positions. Such was the end of the samurai class which had ruled Japan from the late twelfth century.

Along with the abolition of the class system, feudal rules and regulations restricting economic freedom were removed. The samurai class not only became free to engage in productive occupations, they were strongly encouraged to do so. The regulations prohibiting peasants from leaving the countryside and from selling their lands or choosing which crops to raise were abolished. Peasants became free to undertake any activities which would increase their incomes. As for merchants, the feudal regulations which required them to join guilds and which restricted competition were abolished. It now became possible for anyone to start an enterprise in any field. In particular, because the capital of a single merchant was usually too limited to accomplish great achievements in the new period, the government encouraged the formation of joint-stock companies.

Restrictions on domestic transportation and communications were also lifted. Provincial governments had often imposed tariffs on goods imported into their territories and had restricted the goods which could be sold outside, in order to preserve economic order. The Tokugawa shogunate, from the standpoint of internal security, prohibited the construction of bridges at certain rivers and intentionally preserved natural barriers to domestic transportation; it also established checkpoints and required travellers to show permits for travelling. The Meiji government abolished the checkpoints and internal tariffs, and took measures to develop the national network of transportation and communications for the purpose of economic as well as political and social integration of the country. This new policy led to the construction of railways, subsidies to the Mitsubishi *zaibatsu* to establish a modern shipping line, and the establishment of postal and telegraphic services.

Trade with Western countries had resumed in 1859, but under the Tokugawa system, there were various barriers to its expansion. For one, the shogunate and provincial governments took various measures to restrict the sales of commodities to foreign merchants because it threatened their political stability. Also, the extreme nationalists who were determined to expel the 'Western barbarians' interfered with foreign trade by undertaking terrorist attacks. The new Meiji government, on the other hand, made it clear that the country needed to increase contacts with the West in order to gain the new ideas and technical knowledge necessary for modernizing the country. For this purpose, it removed the ban on foreign travel, sent students abroad, etc. Foreign trade was promoted as one aspect of international relations and also as a means to increase the wealth of the country, and the feudal regulations which had impeded the growth of trade at the end of the Tokugawa period were removed.

Economic freedom could not be allowed under the feudal system for two basic reasons. First, the competition accompanying economic freedom would undermine the social fabric of the feudal society which was ascriptive and based on group solidarity. In order to keep the 'anti-social' force of competition in check, various economic restrictions were imposed. At the same time, values which tended to downgrade merchants who resorted to individualistic actions were encouraged. Confucianism (the official ideology of the Tokugawa period) supported such values. In addition, it was felt that to allow certain freedoms to peasants (e.g. the freedom to leave their villages) was inconsistent with the basic tenet of the feudal system in which agriculture is the main economic base. Were such freedoms to be allowed, it would spell the end of agriculture as the dominant industry, and thus, physiocracy (which provided the feudal system a theoretical justification for its 'agriculture first' principle) would have to be replaced by a new economic philosophy. This in turn would entail a new political philosophy, which would necessitate a new form of government. The economic philosophy adopted by the Meiji government was biased in favour of manufacturing industry, but in principle, it considered all industries potentially beneficial to society and left the determination of their relative importance to the market mechanism.

There was a certain consensus among the lower-ranking samurai in the Restoration movement that the Tokugawa political system had to be replaced by one centred upon the emperor as head of the state, but there was considerable difference in opinion as to the extent to which feudal institutions should be retained. The relatively radical social and economic reforms instituted in the early Meiji reflected the view of the so-called 'new intellectuals' who had either studied 'Western Learning' or visited Western countries near the end of the Tokugawa period, and who felt strongly the necessity to reform Japan's social and economic systems along Western lines.[3] A small group of these people formed at the Ministry of Finance in mid-1869, with Okuma Shigenobu as the central figure. This group made a blue-print of the institutional reforms which they felt were necessary for the creation of a modern Japan.

These modernizing intellectuals attributed the economic strength of Western countries to their free economic and social systems, and felt strongly that it was necessary to create a free society if Japan were to become a dynamic country. The economic freedom of the West was supported by the economic doctrine of *laissez-faire* which had become dominant by the mid-nineteenth century. The theory of *laissez-faire* capitalism is usually attributed to Adam Smith, who was, if not the founder of the doctrine, at least its most explicit advocate in the late eighteenth century when government interference in the economy was rampant. Smith argued in the *Wealth of Nations* that a nation's wealth resulted from the diligence and ingenuity of each of its citizens and that these attributes were best guaranteed under free competition. The 'new intellectuals' did not particularly take to his notion of non-interference by the government,[4] but they agreed that a greater degree of competition was necessary to stimulate economic progress in Japan.

Some of the new government's reforms were opposed by certain segments of the population. The loss of social privileges, for example, had been hard for the samurai; even worse was the policy of the new government to reduce financial support for them. After fiefs were abolished, the Meiji government took over the responsibility of paying rice stipends to the samurai, but stipends soon came to occupy too large a share of the budget and seemed certain to interfere with the modernization programme. Therefore, to lessen the dead weight of the past, the government first reduced the amount of rice stipends, and then, a few years later, carried out a compulsory commutation of the stipends to government bonds. Although the consequent interest burden incurred by the government was not light, the interest received by the samurai households ranged from 30 to 40 yen per year on the average, far below the amount needed to support a family. To many lower samurai, it was emotionally difficult to understand why they had to lose the social privileges they had enjoyed because of the success of a movement to which they had greatly contributed. A number of these samurai became inspired to further revolution, once the full scope of the reforms was disclosed, and an opposition bent on violence soon appeared.

At first, the opposition group tried to change government policy by assassinating supporters of the reforms, but this tactic did not alter government policy. From 1874 to 1877, the opposition raised rebellions in western Japan, hoping to overwhelm the central government. The last of the rebellions, the Satsuma Rebellion, headed by Saigo Takamori (himself one of the major architects of the Restoration movement), presented the most serious threat both to the prestige and finances of the new government. The rebellions were suppressed, however, in a relatively short time, and armed resistance to the new government ceased. In retrospect, these rebellions seem to have been unable to challenge the modern army of the new government or to win popular support; in a sense, they seem simply to have been an unavoidable ordeal, given the scope of the radical reforms being carried out.

By Western standards, the 'new intellectuals' of Meiji Japan appear conservative and traditional, especially in view of the autocratic state they later helped establish. Actually, they were but a small minority who had received ideological impulses from the West, and there was a wide gap in outlook between them and the masses—probably as wide as that which exists in the developing countries of the present day. But unlike the intellectuals in those countries (who belong to or have numerous ties to privileged groups which have vested interests in the institutional *status quo*), the 'new intellectuals' of the Meiji Restoration were lower samurai, and very much discontented with the hierarchical and ascriptive feudal society which often negated their talent and ability. It is true that they could have submerged their discontent and resorted to passive retreatism, as often happens under such circumstances, but they translated their discontent into action and spearheaded a movement to establish a more just society.

Contact with the West not only provided Japanese leaders with a model for modernization, it also gave a rationale for institutional reforms. In view of what had happened to China and other Asian countries after the arrival of the Western Powers, it was quite plausible that if no precautionary measures were taken, Japan would become a colony. This Western threat created a sense of urgency, without which it is difficult to understand how such radical reforms could have been accomplished internally in such a short time. On this point, Meiji Japan may again be contrasted with the developing countries of today where, despite the need for institutional reforms to accelerate economic development, no urgency is felt on the part of their leaders.

The Meiji reforms were 'revolutionary' in the sense that they destroyed the feudal system and prepared the way for a new economic and political system, but it is important to note that the new government made efforts to help the samurai make the transition to the new society. Most upper samurai were assured of economic security and given government bonds with which they could support their families rather comfortably. Some of them, the shogun and daimyo in particular, became members of the nobility and continued to enjoy social prestige. For the lower samurai, the government bonds did not provide full support,[5] so many of them used the skills they had acquired through education and experience in the old bureaucracy to become professional soldiers, officials in the central and local governments, policemen, or teachers. If they wanted to start businesses or to undertake land reclamation and settle down as farmers, they were often given subsidies and other forms of government assistance. Furthermore, though they became commoners and equals to former merchants and peasants in all practical ways, society continued to pay lip service to the old class distinctions by calling them *shizoku* (descendants of samurai) to satisfy their need to feel socially different from others. Of course, these measures did not satisfy all samurai, but they at least ameliorated the difficult situation samurai faced in the transition.

The government policy to help former samurai adjust to the new society had some bearing on the nature of the Meiji Restoration. Since it destroyed the feudal system and launched Japan into a modern era, it may be compared to the French or Russian revolutions. Still, there was too much continuity between the new period and the old for it to be considered a true revolution. The old ruling class was not exterminated, nor did the new ruling class come from the ruled class of the former period, as was the case in the French or Russian revolutions. The Meiji Restoration was also incomplete as a social revolution, for many feudal remnants remained in the social structure of the new period. In particular, the social structure of villages, where the bulk of the population lived, was deliberately left intact.

The main reason why the Meiji Restoration was incomplete as a revolution was that it was not a revolution by the ruled, but rather a revolution within the samurai class, and was, in a way, a power struggle within the ruling class.[6] Yet, there was a great difference between those discontented samurai who participated in the rebellions and the 'new intellectuals' who later steered the course of Meiji modernization. The latter wanted to abolish feudal privileges and restrictions and to introduce Western ideas and institutions. In this, they were far more 'revolutionary' than the former, but they were not concerned with sweeping away all pre-modern institutions and values and creating a new society based on égalitarian principles. Nor was this possible in view of the vested interests of their fellow samurai participants in the Restoration movement. As a consequence, the measures they undertook reflect a peculiar mixture of modernizing and conserving strategies.

OCCUPATION REFORMS

The political changes which began in 1945 were the aftermath of the defeat in the Pacific War. The first several months of the war had gone well for Japan: the attack on Pearl Harbor was a severe blow to the Pacific Fleet of the United States, and all South-East Asia had come rapidly under Japanese control. The course of events began to change, however, with the battle of Midway in mid-1942, and turned definitely against Japan after the battle of Guadalcanal. By mid-1944, Japan had lost naval supremacy and was cut off from the overseas territories which had supplied the raw materials necessary for its strategic industries. From then on, Japan's defeat became almost certain, although the war continued for another year. Finally, in August 1945, Japan surrendered unconditionally to the Allies.

The first and foremost task of the Supreme Commander for the Allied Powers (SCAP), who directed the occupation policy, was to destroy the military superstructure that had devastated Asia in general and caused considerable sacrifices on the part of the Allies before their victory. In accordance with this policy, SCAP abolished all military establishments, stopped armament production, and returned all soldiers to the civilian sector. It was also necessary to carry out reforms in the political, economic and social spheres either as punitive measures or to prevent the re-emergence of the military.

In the political realm, 'Tenno-ism' (the system in which the emperor was held to be divine and possessed of absolute power) which had served to support the supremacy of the military was overthrown; the Maintenance of Public Order Act and its watchdog, the special political police, who had terrorized persons or groups who objected to the war, were abolished; and the state was separated from Shintoism which had inculcated xenophobic nationalism and glorified death for the cause of the state. Also, a large number of Japanese leaders who were judged to have actively supported the war were purged from public posts. In the economic sector, the *zaibatsu*, which had collaborated with the military and greatly benefited from it, were dissolved. Land reform was also carried out, first to destroy the economic base of landlords who had supported the military, and also to improve the living condition of peasants lest they turn to violence later. In the social area, educational reform was carried out to stop these teachings which glorified the military and worshipped the emperor; labour reform to develop labour unions into a force capable of preventing the rise of fascism in industry was also enacted.

Although the destruction of the military backbone of Japan was the top priority of SCAP, it was clear from the beginning that a new political system had to be created to replace the old one. The Meiji constitution, which had defined the emperor as sovereign ruler of the country and made it possible for the military to dominate national politics, was replaced by a new democratic constitution which incorporated popular sovereignty, women's suffrage, and the guarantee of fundamental rights. The economic and social reforms needed to destroy the military were also useful in creating institutions to sustain the democratic political system and help it take root in Japanese society. The dissolution of the *zaibatsu* and the land reform spread economic power more evenly over the population, making it more difficult for a small group of people to dominate national politics. Labour reform made it possible for workers to bargain for better pay and working conditions, and to use their organizations for voicing political demands. Educational reform also served the purpose of democracy by teaching democratic values, developing more rational minds, and creating greater opportunities for education.

Of particular interest here are the three economic reforms carried out at this time: land reform, economic de-concentration, and labour reform. The essential feature of the land reform was the transfer of ownership of leased land to cultivating tenants. First, the government bought all leased land held by absentee landlords, and in the case of resident landlords, the land leased in excess of one *cho* (4 *cho* in Hokkaido).[7] The government then sold the land to cultivating tenants. Consequently, the proportion of land under tenant cultivation decreased drastically. From 1941 to 1950, the proportion of leased paddy land decreased from 53 to 11 per cent, and leased upland from 37 to 9 per cent. As for the land which remained in the hands of landlords, leases were made difficult to terminate without the consent of tenants, and rents were commuted to money rent and set in terms of the 1945 official price of rice, well below the market price. At the time of the reform, rents constituted only 10 per cent of the total yield.

The major measure of economic de-concentration was the dissolution of the *zaibatsu*; this was carried out by the Holding Company Liquidation Commission set up in 1946. Mitsubishi, Mitsui, Sumitomo and Yasuda were the largest *zaibatsu*; in addition, there were lesser national *zaibatsu* and local *zaibatsu*. The Commission ordered eighty-three holding companies and fifty-seven *zaibatsu* families to surrender their holdings, which amounted to 233 million shares, and disposed of them in such a way that they could be bought by a large number of individuals and associations. In the process, the holding companies were dissolved, companies which had been under their control became independent, and *zaibatsu* families lost their economic power. Further legislation in 1947 provided that any *zaibatsu* family member holding any official position in a former *zaibatsu* company had to retire and could not return to his former position for ten years.

The second measure of economic de-concentration was the dissolution of all cartels and other control associations formed since 1931 when the Major Industries Control Law was passed. The third was to purge business leaders who had collaborated closely with the military. By mid-1947, about 2,000 persons who had been key officials in major companies during the war had been purged. In December 1947, the Elimination of Excessive Concentration of Economic Power Law was passed, and the Holding Company Liquidation Commission was empowered to break up companies which held excessive economic power. The Commission designated 325 companies, but since there was considerable objection to the law both inside and outside Japan, only eleven companies were broken up.[8] Finally, in March 1948, the Board of Smaller Enterprises was set up to promote the growth of small, efficient and independent companies.

The labour reform started with the passage of the Trade Union Law of 1945, which guaranteed the rights to organize, to bargain collectively and to strike. Two and a half years later, there were about 34,000 unions with a total membership of 6.6 million. Since at no time in the pre-war period had union membership exceeded half a million, the increase in union membership was quite impressive. In 1946, another law was passed to provide a mechanism for settling labour disputes. Then in 1947, three more laws were passed to establish protective labour standards, provide a system of free public employment exchange, and eliminate feudalistic labour practices.

The economic chaos and hyperinflation of the early post-war years provided tremendous opportunities for energetic people to make money but they dealt a severe blow to the rentier class. Their savings were frozen as a measure to maintain the solvency of financial institutions, so as inflation progressed, the real value of savings declined. They also bore the brunt of the capital tax, levied on property of individuals valued in excess of 100,000 yen, which increased from 10 per cent in the first bracket to the maximum of 90 per cent. Landlords lost heavily not only because of the land reform but also as a result of the hyperinflation which caused the value of fixed income from land sale or rent to plummet. Around 1950 when major reforms were completed and economic stabilization restored, a large number of peasants were better off, but at the expense of their former landlords; the dead weight of the rentier class was lighter; and the *nouveaux riches*, who emerged from these chaotic years, constituted a dynamic element within the economy.

One might argue that the rapid growth which followed the occupation can be regarded as sufficient evidence of the contribution of the reforms to post-war economic growth; but in fact the causal relationships are not clearly established. With regard to the Meiji period, there is a consensus that the reforms were an essential step for future economic development, but in the case of the occupation reforms, there is no such consensus. It is sometimes argued that post-war growth did not have anything to do with the reforms, since the purposes of the reforms were often not achieved; and where they were, their impact on economic growth was ambiguous.

The negative perspective on this question may be summarized as follows. In spite of far-reaching effects on the structure of the rural economy, the land reform was not related to agricultural growth. Agricultural production increased mainly because of the development of rice varieties at government experimental stations and the increased production of fertilizer—neither of which had anything to do with the land reform. The de-concentration measures were ineffective in various ways. The Elimination of Excessive Concentration of Economic Power Law was a dead letter from the late 1940s, and was finally repealed in the mid-1950s. As a consequence, large companies completely dominate the economy today. The *zaibatsu* dissolution was also ineffective as can be seen from the pre-eminence of the Mitsubishi, Mitsui and Sumitomo companies, virtually as they were before. Finally, there is the labour reform. The effects of trade unionism are more likely to have been negative (as might be inferred from the case of Britain). Furthermore, the paternalistic employment practices, which the labour reform attempted to eliminate, remained intact in many companies, operating in some ways as a positive factor in economic growth.

Although these arguments have certain validity and demand an explicit specification of causation, the points are not sufficient to negate the contribution of the occupation reforms to post-war economic growth. To take the case of the land reform first, there is no place for it in growth accounting which measures productivity increase in terms of input increase. Unfortunately, such an approach completely ignores the question of motivation—why agricultural inputs increased and why new varieties were readily adopted. The land reform increased the returns to cultivating tenants and eliminated uncertainty concerning the land tenure which had discouraged long-term investment. It seems more reasonable to argue that the land reform increased the motivation of peasants to make the best use of the available technology.

Secondly, the effects of the de-concentration measures were not as far-reaching as those of the land reform; nevertheless, they did contribute to economic de-concentration and the establishment of a competitive framework. The economic groups which emerged in the 1950s—such as Mitsubishi, Mitsui and Sumitomo—and which have played an important role in the economy since then, are quite differently structured from their days as *zaibatsu*. The holding companies which controlled and coordinated *zaibatsu* companies were made illegal, and have not made a comeback. Also, the influence of former *zaibatsu* families on the companies carrying the *zaibatsu* name is completely gone; they are run under modern management systems. Companies in the same group consult each other and coordinate their activities to a certain extent, but the cooperation is very loose in comparison with the *zaibatsu* days when different companies functioned like different departments of the same organization. Actually, it is more important to note the independence present day companies possess in regard to personnel, finance, investment and technology than to emphasize the coordination of their activities.[9] Finally, these three groups (Mitsubishi, Mitsui, Sumitomo) are much less important in the overall national economy than the *zaibatsu* had been in the 1930s—a result of the growth of many other companies in the post-war period.

It may appear that competition is highly restricted and economic efficiency is low today because many industries are oligopolies, but this view is not quite correct. First, since competition with foreign companies in both domestic and export markets put pressures on oligopolies to strive for greater efficiency, the concentration of production cannot be equated with low efficiency. Secondly, the Anti-Monopoly Law, passed during the occupation, makes various practices which restrict competition illegal, and its supervisory body, the Fair Trade Commission, keeps a close watch. Compared with the period when the *zaibatsu* became pre-eminent, it is more difficult today for a company to increase economic power by merger, stockholding or take-over. The Anti-Monopoly Law prevented re-concentration of economic power dispersed during the occupation period, and contributed to the competitive framework of the post-war economy.

When other non-economic reforms are considered, the contribution of post-war institutional reforms to economic growth becomes even more apparent. One indisputable contribution comes from disarmament. From the Meiji up until Japan's defeat in 1945, military expenditure had been an important percentage of government expenditures. Even in peace time, the proportion had been close to 20 per cent, and in war time, which was by no means infrequent, the proportion exceeded 50 per cent.[10] After the defeat, as a result of the fact that Japanese security has been maintained under the American nuclear 'umbrella', by a small self-defence force, the burden of military expenditure has been light. It has declined to a very small percentage of government expenditure, recently never exceeding 1 per cent of GNP.[11] In other words, not only did wasteful expenditure sharply decline, thus making capital available for constructive purposes, but technology and manpower were also released from war industries. In the post-war period, the technology of heavy industry (which had produced such war machines as the Zero fighter plane) became available for the production of non-military goods.[12] Also, the absorption of talented individuals into the military stopped, and they were able to apply their talents to the build-up of the post-war economy.

Furthermore, the occupation reforms favourably affected the overall infrastructure of the economy. This can best be seen by examining first the attributes of a dynamic economic system. In such a system, available human talent is tapped through the best possible educational system, economic organizations make best use of that talent through a meritocracy and rigorous competition. Prima facie, it can be argued that the occupation reforms contributed to the more effective use of talent by creating greater opportunities for education through educational reforms and reduction in income inequality (especially in the rural sector); to the establishment of a meritocracy by inculcating the importance of fairness into the population and by contributing to the separation of management from ownership through removal of *zaibatsu* family influence; and to a more competitive economic system by implementing the dissolution of the *zaibatsu* and other deconcentration measures, and by preparing the way for its integration into the international economy.

So far, the changes which the occupation reforms brought about have been emphasized, but it must be remembered that there was a great deal of continuity between the Japan of 1935 and of 1950. Nevertheless, the changes were too dramatic to have been brought about by internal forces alone. It would be unfair to say that before the war, no Japanese wanted democracy or disarmament, or that no Japanese saw the excesses of the *zaibatsu* or the injustice of land distribution. Still, the fact remains that the Japanese were not able to change the system on their own. The pre-war system was still young, and despite some inconsistencies and weaknesses, it was not close to crumbling under domestic pressure as had been the case with Tokugawa feudalism. Nor was there an immediate need to change the system to meet external threats, since the system itself had been established as a logical extension of the national policy to create 'a strong military'.

This argument seems to imply that once a moderately rational system is established, in spite of internal inconsistencies, it is very difficult for substantial change to take place internally. If strong external pressure is applied, however, such change can take place more quickly, triggering a spurt of economic activity. Unfortunately, this process is bound to involve violence, for institutions which need to be changed are usually built into the power structure of a society and cannot be changed without breaking the backbone of the establishment. If external pressure is weak, there would be no violence, but there would also be only minor changes, if anything. Herein lies the basic dilemma of people who advocate the use of external pressure as a catalyst for institutional reforms in the developing countries of today.

1. The question of whether historical materialism is applicable to the Meiji Restoration is not the same as whether it was a bourgeois revolution, although the two are often confused. The former is a question of whether economic forces explain the Meiji Restoration. Historical materialism is rejected here because it is more natural to consider that the Restoration was brought about by the lower samurai as a political response to the decay of feudalism and the Western challenge. For this view, see, for example, Horie Yasuzo, *Nihon Shihonshugi no Seiritsu* [The establishment of Japanese

ıtalism], Tokyo, Yuhikaku, 1948, Chapter 2 and Sakata Yoshio, *ıeiji Ishin Shi* [History of the Meiji Restoration], Tokyo, Miraisha, 1960. Those who argue that the Meiji Restoration was a bourgeois revolution (as the *Rono* school of Marxist historians do) are on much more shaky ground, for Japanese capitalism was at an incipient stage of development at the mid-nineteenth century.

2. Horie, op. cit., pp. 1–6.

3. Sakata Yoshio calls these people *shin chishikijin* (new intellectuals) in *Shikon Shosai* [Samurai's soul and merchant's acumen], Tokyo, Miraisha, 1964, p. 120.

4. Smith believed that when there was no competition, people tended to become indolent and reluctant to submit themselves to the trouble and inconvenience of altering their habits by adopting new and promising inventions. Thus, he contended that since free competition—a condition indispensable to human progress—was best assured when people were free to pursue their own interests, the role of the government should be to avoid, as much as possible, interference with the free interplay of individual pursuits.

5. The interest income of the average lower samurai was about 30 to 40 yen per year. Noro Eitaro, *Nihon Shihonshugi Hattatsu Shi* [History of the development of Japanese capitalism], Tokyo, Iwanami Shoten, 1954, Iwanami Bunko, p. 141.

6. It can be argued that in this respect, the Meiji Restoration was similar to the American Revolution.

7. One *cho* is equivalent to 2.451 acres, or approximately 1 hectare.

8. For opposition in the United States, see Holding Company Liquidation Commission, *Nihon Zaibatsu to sono Kaitai* [Japanese *zaibatsu* and their liquidation], Tokyo, Hara Shobo, 1951, Vol. I, pp. 316–17.

9. For a discussion on whether or not such groups can be considered *zaibatsu*, see E. Hadley, *Anti-Trust in Japan*, Princeton, Princeton University Press, 1969, Chapter 11. R. Caves and M. Uekusa discuss the nature of group activities in Chapter 4 of *Industrial Organization in Japan*, Washington, The Brookings Institution, 1976.

10. Emi Koichi and Shionoya Yuichi, *Government Expenditure: Estimates of Long Term Economic Statistics of Japan Since 1868*, Vol. 7, Tokyo, Toyo Keizai Shinposha, 1966, Chapter 3.

11. The proportion of military expenditure to GNP was about 2 per cent in 1954, the highest in the post-war period. Since then, it has declined to below 1 per cent.

12. The 'zero' was fully comparable to any fighter the Allies had in 1940–2.

VI

Pathology of Growth

PATHOLOGY OF GROWTH

JAPANESE economic development is, in many ways, a remarkable achievement. After all, it was a resource-poor, feudal, agricultural country that was transformed into a prosperous, industrial nation in a very brief period of time. If, however, it is remembered that Japanese development took a heavy toll of human suffering in the process, unalloyed admiration for Japanese development must undergo considerable qualification. It is tempting to take economic development out of the historical context to look at it alone, but since the dark side of Japan's modernization was an inextricable part of its economic development, such an approach is not justified. Thus, to attempt to give a balanced view, this chapter discusses first the negative aspects of Japanese development, and second the question of how these negative aspects affect the applicability of the Japanese development model to other countries.

Although economic development brings about a rise in the standard of living for the average person, some are always left out or harmed in the process of development. For them, economic development is an anguish rather than a blessing. Factory workers may be cited as an example. In the early phase of industrial development, factories were dirty, and in summertime unbearably hot and humid places. Workers could take Sundays off, but during the remaining six days of the week, their normal work load was twelve to fifteen hours per day. They were also often forced to work for a few extra hours. When they became sick, they could not always rest because of various pressures applied by their employers. In the worst cases, gangsters were employed to 'discipline' workers. In the contemporary period, when workers are not satisfied with the employment situation, they can at least quit, but in the prewar period, young workers were often indentured by their parents and did not have the right to quit until the term of indenture expired. Most workers endured horrible working conditions trying to make the best of the circumstances, but many died by industrial accidents or diseases, and enjoyed none of the fruits of industrial progress. For these people, the factory was hell.[1]

The evils of Japanese economic development are not confined only to the worker. Its critics would point, as a second example, to the extreme poverty of many people in the midst of increased prosperity. Those who have done well in economic competition have been rewarded, but the losers have been severely punished. One group of 'losers' were tenants in villages. They were the poorest among the rural population, and their economic hardship is well documented. It is important to note, however, that the problem of tenancy did not originate in the modern period; the same problem existed also in the Tokugawa and in earlier periods. One might argue that there is no clear evidence that the condition of tenants worsened after the Meiji Restoration, but at least in two respects the problem became more serious. In the Tokugawa period, the relationship between tenants and landlords was social as well as economic, and economic factors alone did not determine land tenure. After the Meiji Restoration, as a consequence of the increased power of landlords under the new property law, the land tenure of many tenants was shortened and became less certain. The increased rate of tenancy was the other serious problem. Towards the end of the Tokugawa period, the rate was somewhere around 30 per cent, but by the mid-1930s, it had increased to roughly

45 per cent.[2] This increased rate of tenancy caused some concern about land productivity, but it was also a serious social problem. A large number of peasants were tied down to a subsistence income and were not able to enjoy the benefits of agricultural development.

In major cities, there were large slum areas which did not diminish significantly for at least the first several decades of economic development. Again, the problem of slums was not unique to the modern period, and it can be argued that economic development wiped out several slum areas. Still, most old slums remained and some new ones were created. Some of the inhabitants enjoyed equal opportunities for education, but because of their lack of effort, incompetence or misfortune, drifted to slums: for them there may be little room for sympathy. Since many slum inhabitants were illiterate, however, they could not make rational plans, nor could they adjust to changes in economic circumstances. They participated in economic competition with little preparation, and from the beginning, their chances were nil. Forming the marginal stratum of the population, they lived in crowded shacks and were tied to subsistence living. To make the situation worse, in order to escape temporarily from their miserable conditions, many of them drank and gambled on money borrowed at usurious rates of interest from moneylenders. This created a vicious circle of poverty, and for most people, exit from the slums was permanently closed. Certainly, they could be considered losers in the economic system; because they were members of the Japanese nation, they had the right to enjoy a standard of living commensurate with the productive capacity of the country. The economic system which brought about their plight can be rightly blamed.[3]

Japanese economic development is also at the root of environmental disruption (pollution and noise). While this is not a uniquely Japanese phenomenon, the problem is most serious there. The mental as well as physical health of many Japanese is affected by noise, air and water pollution. Noise is a serious problem in the vicinity of airports and along the train routes. Water in some parts of Japan is polluted with cadmium, mercury and other poisonous chemicals. Air in major cities and near industrial complexes is polluted with carbon monoxide, sulphurous acid gas, nitric oxide and lead compounds which cause asthma, bronchitis and lung cancer. To a certain extent, the pollution problem originated from the high population density of the country which made the relocation of houses and effective city planning difficult. However, a large part of the responsibility falls upon the unconscionable enterprises which pursued private profits and ignored the social costs of production, and upon the government which allowed business interest to dictate environmental policy.

The most publicized effect of environmental disruption has been the mercury poisoning at Minamata in Kyushu. Fish in the sea around Minamata were poisoned by the organic mercury discharged by a chemical factory in the city. Many fishermen and their families in the area became sick after having eaten poisonous fish over the years. About 100 of them later died, and another 600 still remain sick. Many of those who are still alive cannot walk, hear or see properly, and some are totally incapacitated. The chemical factory may not have caused the poisoning intentionally, but it could have stopped the discharge of mercury much earlier when the ill effects on the human body were first brought to its attention and thus reduced the number of victims and the extent of their suffering. It was also regrettable that the government, the Ministry of International Trade and Industry in particular, objected to precautionary measures for fear that approval of such measures might necessitate re-evaluation of its overall policy, thereby adversely affecting industrial production within the country as a whole. The government allowed the factory to continue discharging mercury for almost ten years after the causal relationship between the discharge and poisoning was pointed out by a medical team. Apart from ideological disputes as to the nature of Japanese economic development, even to those concerned with the pollution problem on a purely humanitarian basis, Minamata disease is a clear example of a crime committed by the establishment.

It is sometimes argued that these problems of Japanese economic development could have been avoided if a socialist economic system had been adopted. The miserable working conditions in factories, exploitation of workers, mal-distribution of income, the presence of a fairly large marginal population, and serious pollution problems are, in many ways, the excesses of capitalistic development. Unlike capitalism, socialism is committed to égalitarian principles and the welfare of workers; it attempts to avoid the problems arising from external diseconomy (such as the pollution problem) by centralizing economic decision making. To advocates of socialism, capitalism is immoral, inhumane, and exploitative.

If the Japanese economic system had been socialist, there is strong reason to believe that the growth rate in the past century would have been much slower. Japan is poor in natural resources and suffers from a high population density with the result that it has to import primary products and food from foreign countries in order to increase the standard of living. To pay for this import bill, Japan has to export manufactured goods. In an important way, Japan's standard of living depends on the terms and volume of trade. There is little Japan can do with regard to the former, but the latter depends on Japan's competitiveness in the international market, which is in turn determined by industrial efficiency.

Industrial efficiency is more likely to be guaranteed in a system in which success is rewarded and failure punished. In capitalism, firms which increase output when demand expands or reduce the costs of production through inventiveness or the introduction of better technology developed elsewhere, are rewarded with profits; those which fail to be adaptive and innovative suffer losses, or if they continue to do so, they will be phased out of the economic scene. The fear of failure in competitive struggle and the expectation of reward in the case of success arouse the productiveness and inventiveness of the firm.

The basic problem of socialism, as observed in the Soviet Union and the People's Republic of China, is that there is no such fear or expectation. Their economic systems are bureaucratized and politicized, and economic decisions are made by the state which is often immune to the law of supply and demand. Managers at production sites are often political appointees, who are best qualified as political entrepreneurs. Usually, technological progress is slow, and production is wasteful in socialist states.

The economic inefficiency of socialist states is well demonstrated in international trade. In the trade between socialist and capitalist nations, there are few manufactured goods the socialist nations can sell to the capitalist nations. Exports from socialist nations consist predominantly of primary products. On the other hand, a large quantity of industrial goods are sold by the capitalist nations to socialist nations. Also, in the developing areas, the socialist nations cannot compete successfully with the capitalist nations in industrial exports. In Latin America, Africa and South Asia, capitalist nations provide the bulk of imported industrial goods.

The fact that economic efficiency is more likely under capitalism is still not sufficient justification for the excesses of Japanese economic development. The relevant question to be posed is whether there is an economic system which ensures economic efficiency, and at the same time, avoids the excesses pointed out above. To some economists, avoiding such excesses and maintaining high efficiency at the same time are incompatible concepts; in other words, if the excesses are to be avoided, economic efficiency must be sacrificed. However, since Sweden has succeeded in achieving a fairly high growth despite large welfare expenditures, it seems possible to devise an economic system which would meet the above requirements. This question is particularly relevant for developing countries considering the future course of their economic systems.

Another objection to Japanese economic development comes from people who argue that development may have increased the level of economic welfare but it has not made the Japanese people happier. Certainly there is no question that many sources of unhappiness have been eliminated by economic development: freedom from famine, better nutrition, prolonged life expectancy, better housing, increased leisure time, better education, better medical care, better communication and transportation facilities, and increased employment opportunities are prominent examples. Yet, economic development has also created new problems, such as fear of competition, fear of bankruptcy, boredom at repetitive simple work, and adjustment problems in hierarchical corporate structures, not to mention industrial sickness, industrial accidents, and the pollution, noise, etc., discussed above. To some people, it is not clear what proportion economic development occupies on a scale of human happiness.

If one views that improvement in material life is a small part of human happiness, the usefulness of stressing economic development becomes questionable. In this view, even if the material standard of life were sacrificed, questions such as the following must be answered, in order to give a balanced view on economic development. Would individuals be happier going back to pollution-free agriculture and working at their own pace rather than working at factories under supervision? Would life be better if more attention were paid to spiritual pursuits? Does the desire for material progress not originate in greed? And does economic development not augment a person's greed, and consequently, bring about an unhappy world?

In this view, human progress must be measured in terms of gains in general happiness.

The opposite view maintains that it is useless to consider the problem of happiness because no matter how many difficulties are surmounted or how many ideals are realized, humans have an unlimited capacity for misery. In spite of vast achievements in the past, nothing proves that happiness has increased over time. Nor is there any possibility that it will increase in the future since it is unlikely that human nature will change. Critics of material progress seem to feel that people would become happier by taking up spiritual pursuits, but there is no such guarantee—constant contemplation of spiritual things could just as well lead to great unhappiness. Therefore, according to this view, it is best not to deal with the question of happiness in connexion with the subject of economic development.

To most of those economists who are practically oriented, the question of happiness is too vague to be useful. For many people outside economics, however, this question is important, and they demand that it be answered. At present, there is no methodology for incorporating the question of happiness into a study of economic development, but as long as material progress cannot be equated with an increase in happiness, every time economic development becomes an important social goal, the question of its ultimate objectives will be raised.

This question has been of philosophical interest in Japan, but apparently not to the Meiji leaders. If they had pondered over it, they probably would have seen no contradiction between increased happiness and economic development; in their minds happiness probably depended upon national glory, and economic development was seen as the most desirable way to achieve it. More likely, however, they did not consider the problem seriously. Since Western Powers were pursuing a policy of Realpolitik, threatening the independence of East Asian nations, the Meiji leaders likely did not have the leisure time to contemplate the question of whether or not economic development would enhance human happiness. To them, development was a necessity for survival. Whether or not a country is able to consider the problem of human happiness in conjunction with economic development is often dictated by the international environment it faces.

THE COST OF IMPERIALISM

The Japanese military expansion not only killed, maimed or otherwise injured a large number of soldiers, but it also inflicted severe hardship on the entire rest of the country. In its early phase (the period up to the end of the Sino-Japanese War (1894–5)), the human costs of warfare were smaller; since the duration of war was short, battles were fought in restricted areas, and the destructive capability of weapons was still limited. For example, the number of soldiers killed in the Sino-Japanese War was about 17,000. In the next war, the Russo-Japanese War (1904–5), human sacrifice escalated: about 100,000 Japanese soldiers died. Even this, however, was small compared with the death of 2.3 million soldiers and 660,000 civilians during the Pacific War.[4]

There were also other dimensions to the human cost of war. An unknown number of people were crippled and disabled. Still many others suffered from diseases, such as radiation poisoning, contracted during the war. Considerable psychological damage was also inflicted upon parents who lost sons, wives who lost husbands, and children who lost fathers. Furthermore, there was the suffering of people who held views in opposition to government policy. Many of these people were sent to jail by the special police and some died from torture or prolonged imprisonment.

Japanese military expansion also exacted sacrifice from the conquered. In the colonies of Taiwan and Korea, the indigenous people were the object of contempt to the

Japanese, and they were discriminated against in education, employment, promotion, salary, housing and many other matters. After the Pacific War began, many Taiwanese and Koreans were either drafted to fight for Japan or sent to work for low pay in mines and other places in Japan where hard work was required. Trucks, horses and other properties were commandeered and local workers were often used for corvée.

In the countries occupied after 1937, the Japanese arrival brought about economic and political dislocation. In some cases, this contributed to the eventual rise of nationalism and political independence, but the number of atrocities Japanese soldiers committed during their occupation angered many people. Their underlying feeling of superiority towards other Asians coupled with the desire for revenge after a hard fight seem to have caused some Japanese soldiers to take leave of their senses briefly to plunder, murder, torture and rape in the newly conquered countries. The most notorious were the atrocities committed at Nanking in South China. When Japanese soldiers moved into the city chasing defeated Chinese soldiers, they pillaged stores, raped the women, set buildings on fire, and variously killed several hundred thousand Chinese. Manila and Singapore suffered similar fates, although the scale of the atrocities was somewhat smaller.

When did the imperialism which exacted such a high human toll begin? Some consider the Pacific War the only imperialistic war of which Japan can be rightly accused, and thus see it as an aberration from the normal course of Japan's modern history. This apologetic view is convenient if the negative aspects of Japanese modernization are to be minimized, but the truth seems to be more likely that Japanese imperialism began under the Meiji government. There seems to be a common thread of imperialist intention in the wars from the Taiwan expedition of 1874 to the Pacific War. Certainly it is true that when Japan undertook the Taiwan expedition, it was not historically predetermined that Japan would plunge into a series of wars in the subsequent years. The actual course of historical events was determined by a complex interplay of domestic and international forces which evolved over time. Nevertheless, the Taiwan expedition set the imperialist trend which culminated in World War II.

Imperialism as an ideology existed in the late Tokugawa period, and such scholars as Yoshida Shoin (1830–59) argued that Japan should enhance its national power by conquering Korea, Manchuria and China. This expansionist ideology was adopted by the Meiji leaders, who, having emerged from the former warrior class, were naturally inclined toward the view that the weak were destined to be ruled by the strong. Accordingly, in 1874, the first overseas expedition was sent to Taiwan. But Taiwan was not the major target: it was Korea which occupied the minds of Meiji leaders and made them decide to fight two major wars. After Korea was reasonably secure, North China became the next major target.

If the imperialism of the 1930s was significantly different from the earlier experience, it was due to the fact that militarism was rampant in the 1930s. Even so, the problem was rooted in the Meiji era when military command became independent from cabinet control, and when the restriction that the Minister of the Army must be a general and the Minister of the Navy an admiral became firmly established. At first, military excesses were checked because both political and military leaders were united by personal bonds which had been created in the movement for Restoration. As time passed, however, these bonds loosened and it became exceedingly difficult for the civilian government to restrain the military. A large part of the responsibility for imperialist activities therefore must be attributed to the Meiji government which placed too strong an emphasis on the military in creating a modern nation.

It might be argued, however, that Japan had no alternative in those years when the Western Powers were threatening the independence of Asian nations with superior military forces. They had wrested territories and various concessions from China by the time of the Meiji Restoration. Then, in the 1880s, France colonized Indo-China, England expanded its colonial rule in Burma, and Russia decided to construct the trans-Siberian railroad for the purpose of eastward expansion. Faced with the thrust of the Western Powers into Asia, Meiji leaders judged that the survival of the fittest was the law of international relations and acted accordingly.[5]

It might have been possible for the Meiji leaders to have built up a military force for defence purposes but never to have used it for aggression. It was also to ask only for future trouble to impose what they themselves had not liked (unequal treaties and territorial concessions) on neighbouring countries. They could have championed Asian nationalism and helped Asian nations defend their independence from the threat of Western domination. In retrospect, pacifism was not a philosophy which would have necessarily led to national ruin, as they believed. Rather than to Prussia, they might have paid close attention to Switzerland and Sweden, countries which had prospered without foreign conquest, but such was the samurai mentality. The course Japan has followed in the post World War II period was not, by any means, closed to Meiji Japan. In fact, some scholars and journalists at the time argued for such a course, but their views were brushed aside in favour of the expansionist ideology.

Who was responsible for imperialism? According to the materialist interpretation of history, the bourgeoisie was the major architect of imperialism. There is no question but that as economic development progressed after the Restoration, the bourgeoisie increased in power and came to participate in some political decisions. Also, support of the bourgeoisie was important for both political and military leaders: the former needed contributions to finance political campaigning, intrigue, and the build-up of their political influence, whereas the latter needed money to finance military escalation and overseas adventures. Leaders among the bourgeoisie were asked to co-operate, and they used the opportunity to increase their profits as well as political influence, but they were never at the helm of major political and military decisions. Legislatures and elections existed, of course, in pre-war Japan, but the political system was an absolute monarchy in which sovereignty rested with the emperor. The state was essentially run by those who had direct access to him, and most were military men or aristocrats who could in no way be considered the puppets of the bourgeoisie.[6]

The leading decision makers were not bound by popular sentiment, although they could not completely ignore it. Military leaders needed in particular the support of the nation for their expansionist policies. Thus, they appealed to the bourgeoisie on the grounds that expansion of the sphere of Japan's political influence would result in an increased share of profits; to land-hungry peasants they suggested that conquest of foreign territories would provide more land for them to cultivate. They also undertook propaganda campaigns to intensify chauvinistic nationalism. Up to the beginning of the Pacific War, imperialism brought about concrete benefits and won the approval of a large number of Japanese. Without their support, it would have been impossible for the military to have become a dominant force in pre-war Japanese history.

Did imperialism benefit the Japanese economy? Imperialist activities resulted in various concrete economic benefits. For example, territorial expansion eased the pressures on the land which had built up because of population increase. Reparations obtained after the Sino-Japanese War made it possible for Japan to adopt the gold standard and also to construct the Yahata Steel Mill, the first large-scale integrated steel mill in Japan. The various commercial concessions Japan obtained by the actual demonstration or threat of force promoted the country's export industry. Primary products, such as sugar, pulp, iron ore, etc., were brought back to Japan either at concessionary rates or without compensation. Further, militarization required domestic production of armaments and basic materials, and thus became the driving force for the development of heavy industry.

At the same time, imperialism made certain demands on the economy. A significant portion of the nation's manpower was removed from the economy and wasted in the production of military weapons. Capital badly needed for economic development was diverted to military build-up. The high proportion of military expenditure in the government budget retarded development of the infrastructure. Finally, the destruction of property and the economic dislocation which occurred throughout the Pacific War were heavy blows to the economy.

If the overall effects of imperialism in 1945 are judged, it seems that imperialism was more harmful than beneficial. Because of it, the economy was ruined and the country was threatened with the possibility of nationwide famine. If the same type of judgement is made on the 1930s or earlier, however, the task is more difficult because the costs of imperialism were not as overwhelming as in 1945. The costs must be weighed against the benefits over time, which involves a complicated computation. Definite stands are sometimes taken on this issue without taking into consideration both sides of the ledger, but such stands are usually based on either subjective, emotional judgements or illogical reasoning. For example, to infer that Japan would not have purposely pursued a policy harmful to itself, and therefore, imperialism must have been beneficial, is not acceptable since it ignores possible non-economic objectives of imperialism, such as national glory. It is also difficult to accept the inference that the course of development would have remained essentially the same if the expansionist policy had not been pursued, for the militarism which gave rise to the expansionist policy was, in various ways, a dynamic force of modernization, inextricably interwoven with economic and other historical developments in the pre-war period.

CAN JAPAN BE A MODEL OF DEVELOPMENT?

In order for Japan to be taken as a model of development for other countries, all aspects of its historical development must be applicable, for non-economic events cannot be neatly separated from economic processes. For example, imperialism and economic development were so interwoven in the pre-war period that if the latter seems acceptable as a model, some value judgements must inevitably be passed on the former. For those who deplore the destructive features of imperialism, the Japanese experience in the pre-war period serves as a caution rather than as a model.

It is also important to note that economic development in Japan in the pre-war period occurred within a traditional setting, which, in effect, meant that feudal values and institutions remained to a considerable degree. What makes this particularly objectionable is the fact that to a large extent, the feudal remnants were consciously preserved by the state, at the expense of fundamental human rights, equity and democratic values. Economic development under such circumstance is clearly objectionable to those who give great weight to democratic ideals.

Those who would like to take Japanese economic development as a model usually focus on economic performance and tend to ignore the non-economic aspects of modernization. Is this approach wrong? If they argue that, irrespective of political and social developments, the same economic performance could have taken place, their theory is not acceptable. If, however, they simply argue that considerable weight must be given to economic performance, then the acceptability becomes a matter of one's philosophy. For example, if one argues that, since human society does not change in a revolutionary way, it is natural that a considerable amount of traditional heritage remains during the process of economic development and that economic growth should be given greater weight than the achievement of democratic ideals, their viewpoint will be acceptable to a certain limited group of people.

Critics of economic growth tend to underestimate its importance. They disparage those who support it, and employ sarcastic terms to downgrade the emphasis on quantitative over qualitative change.[7] Nevertheless, the unhappiness which economic growth can eliminate or at least reduce should be given proper weight. Poverty is not an admirable economic condition. If economic growth can eliminate poverty, it may be acceptable to a large number of people even if achieved within a traditional (or even totalitarian) setting.

To those who believe in the socialist model of development, or to those who give the greatest weight to democratic ideals, there is little the Japanese experience offers, for Japanese economic development was capitalistic development initiated by a totalitarian state. Perhaps Japanese economic development can be a model only to those who accept capitalism and take a non-revolutionary approach to economic development. Even in such instances, however, the historical process as a whole should not serve as a model, for destructive imperialism and other objectionable events were an inextricable part of it. In the last analysis, it appears that the most which can be expected from the Japanese experience is the light it sheds on certain universal problems of economic development.

1. This paragraph is based on Hosoi Wakizo, *Joko Aishi* [The pitiful history of female workers], Tokyo, Iwanami Shoten, 1954, Iwanami Bunko.

2. Hirano Yoshitaro, *Nihon Shihonshugi Shakai no Kiko* [The mechanism of capitalistic society in Japan], Tokyo, Iwanami Shoten, 1934, p. 68.

3. This paragraph is based on Yokoyama Gennosuke, *Nihon no Kaso Shakai* [The lower strata of Japanese society], Tokyo, Iwanami Shoten, 1949, Iwanami Bunko.

4. Statistical data and historical facts in this section are based on Inoue Kiyoshi, *Nihon Teikokushugi no Keisei* [Formation of Japanese imperialism], Tokyo, Iwanami Shoten, 1968 and Ienaga Saburo, *Taiheiyo Senso* [The Pacific War], Tokyo, Iwanami Shoten, 1968. In English, there are various writings on Japanese imperialism. For example, J. Halliday, *A Political History of Japanese Capitalism*, New York, Pantheon Books, 1975 and J. Dower, 'E. H. Norman, Japan and the Uses of History' in J. Dower (ed.), *Origins of the Modern Japanese State: Selected Writings of E. H. Norman*, New York, Pantheon Books, 1975.

5. Sakata Yoshio, 'Nihon Kindaika no Shuppatsu to Tenkai' [The 'Take Off' and Expansion of Japan's Modernization], *The Jinbun Gakuho*, March 1970, p. 15.

6. Even some Marxist historians (notably those who belong to the *Koza* school) admit that Japanese capitalism was still immature and reject the view that the bourgeoisie controlled political and military power in pre-war Japan. In fact they argue that Japanese capitalism was brought up under protection and guidance of the government. For example, see Hirano Yoshitaro, op. cit., p. 285.

7. For the sarcastic view of economic growth, see R. Mortimer (ed.), *Showcase State: The Illusion of Indonesia's 'Accelerated Modernization'*, London, Angus and Robertson, 1973, Chapter 3.

Glossary

Daimyo: Daimyo were vassals to the shogun, and their domains were called *han*.

Dutch Learning: The study of Western science and the West in general was called *rangaku* (Dutch learning) in the Tokugawa period, since all such study was based on Dutch books (the Dutch were the only ones allowed to trade with Japan during the period of isolation). Dutch learning became popular from about 1740, and progress in subsequent years prepared Japan intellectually for the contact with the West which resumed in the mid-nineteenth century.

Edo: The former name of Tokyo. Edo castle (now the Imperial Palace) was the headquarters of the Tokugawa shogunate.

Han: The *han* were the domains, or fiefs, granted by the shogun to his vassals, the daimyo. The *han* governments had virtual autonomy over internal matters.

Land reform: Used to refer primarily to the reform carried out in the post World War II occupation as an égalitarian measure. It drastically reduced the proportion of tenant cultivated land, and the rent of the tenant cultivated land which remained became only nominal.

Land tax: Used to refer primarily to the first major tax instituted by the Meiji government. It accounted for the bulk of the tax revenue in the first few decades of the Meiji era, and served as a means for the government to channel surpluses from agriculture to industry. Furthermore, since it was a monetary tax (payable only in money), it accelerated the spread of monetary exchanges in villages, and thus, contributed to capitalistic development in rural Japan.

Matsukata deflation: The deflation of the early 1880s named after the then Minister of Finance, Matsukata Masayoshi, who was the prime mover behind the policy. It restored the convertibility of paper notes and laid the foundation for financial orthodoxy in subsequent years.

Meiji era: The reign of the Meiji Emperor (1868–1911) is known as the Meiji era. That of the succeeding Emperor Taisho (1912–25) is called the Taisho era. Similarly, the reign of the present emperor (1926 to the present, the longest reign in history) is called the Showa era.

Meiji Restoration: The Meiji Restoration usually refers to the political events of 1868 which removed the Tokugawa family from the position of shogun and returned supreme power to the emperor, who took the reign name Meiji (meaning 'enlightened rule').

Occupation period: The period from September 1945 to April 1952, during which Japan was occupied by the Allied Powers (principally the U.S.). In September 1951, the San Francisco Peace Treaty was signed, and in April 1952, Japan regained independence.

Rice tax: The rice tax comprised the bulk of government revenues in the Tokugawa period. The tax rate was set by the individual domains, and samurai received their stipends in rice.

Samurai: Samurai, or warriors, were the ruling class in the Tokugawa period, and enjoyed various social privileges over other classes. Towards the end of the period, however, the lower ranking samurai came under straitened circumstances, causing dissension in samurai ranks. Altogether, samurai constituted about 5 per cent of the total population in those days.

Sankin kotai: *Sankin kotai* is the 'hostage' system invented by the founder of the Tokugawa dynasty, Ieyasu, under which the daimyo were required to be in attendance upon the shogun during alternate years.

SCAP: The Supreme Commander of Allied Powers (SCAP) presided over the Japanese government and directed the reforms of the occupation period. General Douglas MacArthur held the position from September 1945 to April 1951, the crucial years of the occupation period, and left his imprint on the institutions of the post-war nation.

Shogun: The shogun was the leading member of the Tokugawa family who exercised absolute rule over both his own clan and the country. His office was called the shogunate.

Tenno: The Emperor of Japan. In the Meiji Constitution, sovereignty rested with him. After World War II, the institution was 'de-mythologized' and he became a figurative head of state.

Tokugawa period: The period of rule under the Tokugawa family (1603–1867).

Zaibatsu: The *zaibatsu* were family controlled groups of monopolistic companies in key fields (banking, trading, mining, shipping and heavy industry). The four largest *zaibatsu* in the pre-war period were those of the Mitsui, Mitsubishi, Sumitomo and Yasuda families. The *zaibatsu* were dissolved as a measure of economic democratization during the occupation period. The Mitsui, Mitsubishi, and Sumitomo groups which exist today should be regarded as some sort of alliance which was formed for mutual benefit, instead of as the cohesive group whose whole operation (production, marketing, finance, personnel decisions, etc.) is controlled by a single person or body, as was the case with the *zaibatsu*.

Chronological Table

LATE TOKUGAWA PERIOD

1853	Commodore Matthew C. Perry arrives.
1854	Signing of the Treaty of Kanagawa. The period of isolation ends.
1858	Signing of the Treaties with Five Nations (commercial treaties).
1859	Trade with the West begins.

MEIJI ERA

1868	The Meiji Restoration.
1869	Institutional reforms begin.
1871	The yen is made the basic unit of money.
1873	Institution of the land tax.
1874	The Saga rebellion–the first armed rebellion against the new government. The first invasionary expedition (against Taiwan) is sent out.
1876	Compulsory commutation of samurai stipends to government bonds.
1877	The Satsuma rebellion, led by Saigo Takamori.
1881	Matsukata Masayoshi becomes Minister of Finance. The Matsukata deflation begins.
1886	Convertibility of paper notes is restored.
1894	The Sino-Japanese War begins.
1895	End of the Sino-Japanese War. Taiwan becomes a Japanese colony.
1897	Gold standard adopted.
1901	Yahata Steel begins production.

1904 Russo-Japanese War begins.

1905 End of the Russo-Japanese War. Russia cedes the southern half of Sakhalin, and recognizes Korea as being within Japan's sphere of interest.

1910 Korea is annexed.

1911 Japan regains tariff autonomy.

TAISHO ERA

1914 World War I begins.

1915 Economic boom begins in Japan.

1917 Japan goes off the gold standard by imposing an embargo on gold exports.

1918 World War I ends.

1920 Post-war recession begins.

1923 The Kanto earthquake—most of Tokyo is destroyed.

SHOWA ERA

1927 Financial crisis.

1930 Japan returns to the gold standard (January).

1931 The Manchuria Incident. The gold standard is abandoned (December).

1937 The China Incident. Transition to a mobilization economy begins.

1941 Pacific War begins with Japan's attack on Pearl Harbor.

1945 Japan accepts unconditional surrender in August. Occupation by the Allies begins in September. General Douglas MacArthur, Supreme Commander for the Allied Powers, launches post-war institutional reforms.

1946 The new constitution (the Showa Constitution) is proclaimed.

1949 Foreign exchange rate set at 360 yen per US dollar.

1950	The Korean conflict begins and triggers the first economic boom in post-war Japan.
1951	Signing of the San Francisco Peace Treaty. Cease-fire for the Korean conflict arranged.
1952	Japan regains independence in April.
1953	Armistice for the Korean conflict signed.
1960	Income Doubling Plan adopted. Decade of high growth begins.
1970	Pollution first becomes a serious social issue.
1971	New exchange rate of 308 yen per US dollar is set in December.
1973	Flexible exchange rate system adopted. The yen starts to revalue. The oil crisis occurs in October, and this triggers a prolonged economic recession.
1974	GNP growth becomes negative for the first time in the post-war period.
1978	The yen is sharply revalued, and in mid-year, the exchange rate drops below 200 yen per US dollar.

Bibliography

The following is a selective list of major writings in English on Japanese economic development. Its purpose is to suggest references for further reading and to elucidate the different interpretations on some of the controversial areas in this field.

CHAPTER I

Ohkawa, K. and Rosovsky, H., *Japanese Economic Growth*, Stanford, Stanford University Press, 1973, pp. 1–43 and 215–50.

———, 'A Century of Japanese Economic Growth', in W. Lockwood (ed.), *The State and Economic Enterprise in Japan*, Princeton, Princeton University Press, 1965.

Patrick, H. and Rosovsky, H., 'Japan's Economic Performance: An Overview', in H. Patrick and H. Rosovsky (eds.), *Asia's New Giant*, Washington, The Brookings Institution, 1976.

CHAPTER II

(a) HIGH GROWTH

Kuznets, S., *Economic Growth of Nations*, Cambridge, Harvard University Press, 1971, Chapter 1.

Ohkawa, K. and Rosovsky, H., op. cit., Chapter 8.

(b) POPULATION GROWTH

Taueber, I., 'Population and Labor Force in the Industrialization of Japan, 1850–1950', in S. Kuznets, W. Moore, and J. Spengler (eds.), *Economic Growth: Brazil, India, Japan*, Durham, North Carolina, Duke University Press, 1955.

(c) DEVELOPMENT WITH OWN RESOURCES

Lockwood, W., *Economic Development of Japan* (expanded edition), Princeton, Princeton University Press, 1968 (various pages) (see 'foreign borrowing' and 'foreign business investment in Japan' in the index).

Komiya, R., 'Direct Investment in Postwar Japan', P. Drysdale (ed.), *Direct Investment in Asia and the Pacific*, Canberra, Australian National University Press, 1972.

Peck, M., 'Technology', in H. Patrick and H. Rosovsky (eds.), op. cit.

(d) TRADITIONAL SETTING

Abbeglen, J., *Japanese Factory*, Glencoe, Illinois, Free Press, 1958, Chapter 8.

Nakayama, I., *Industrialization of Japan*, Honolulu, University Press of Hawaii, 1965, pp. 25–63.

(e) THE ROLE OF THE STATE

Rosovsky, H., *Capital Formation in Japan*, Glencoe, Illinois, Free Press, 1961, Chapter 2.

Trezise, P., 'Politics, Government, and Economic Growth in Japan', in H. Patrick and H. Rosovsky (eds.), op. cit.

Lockwood, W., op. cit., pp. 499–592.

CHAPTER III

Ohkawa, K. and Rosovsky, H., op. cit., pp. 173–95.

Lockwood, W., op. cit., Chapters 6 and 7.

Krause, L. and Sekiguchi, S., 'Japan and the World Economy', in H. Patrick and H. Rosovsky (eds.), op. cit.

CHAPTER IV

(a) CONTRAST WITH CHINA, SOUTH ASIA AND WESTERN EUROPE

Baran, P., *The Political Economy of Growth*, New York, Monthly Review Press, 1957, pp. 151–61.

Geertz, C., *Agricultural Involution*, Berkeley, University of California Press, 1963, pp. 130–54.

Embree, J., 'Thailand–A Loosely Structured Social System', in H. Evers (ed.), *Loosely Structured Social Systems: Thailand in Comparative Perspective*, Southeast Asian Studies, Yale University, 1969.

Lockwood, W., 'Japan's Response to the West–the Contrast with China', *World Politics*, October 1965.

Landes, D., 'Japan and Europe: Contrast in Industrialization', in W. Lockwood (ed.), *The State and Economic Enterprise in Japan*, Princeton, Princeton University Press, 1965.

(b) INITIAL CONDITIONS

Dore, R., *Tokugawa Education*, Berkeley, University of California Press, 1965, Chapters 1 and 10.

Hall, J., 'The Nature of Traditional Society: Japan', in R. Ward and D. Rustow (eds.), *Political Modernization in Japan and Turkey*, Princeton, Princeton University Press, 1964.

———, 'The New Look of Tokugawa History', in J. Hall and M. Jansen (eds.), *Studies in the Institutional History of Early Modern Japan*, Princeton, Princeton University Press, 1967.

Bellah, R., *Tokugawa Religion*, Glencoe, Illinois, Free Press, 1957, Chapters 1 and 7.

Sheldon, C., *The Rise of the Merchant Class in Tokugawa Japan, 1600–1868*, New York, Augustin, 1958, pp. 165–75.

Smith, T., *Agrarian Origins of Modern Japan*, Stanford, Stanford University Press, 1959, pp. 201–13.

Yamamura, K., 'Toward a Re-examination of the Economic History of Tokugawa Japan, 1600–1867', *The Journal of Economic History*, September 1973.

Broadridge, S., 'Economic and Social Trends in Tokugawa Japan', *Modern Asian Studies*, 8.3, 1974.

CHAPTER V

(a) MEIJI RESTORATION AND MEIJI REFORMS

Akamatsu, P., *Meiji 1868: Revolution and Counter-Revolution in Japan*, New York, Harper and Row, 1962.

Beasley, W. G., *The Meiji Restoration*, Stanford, Stanford University Press, 1972.

Jansen, M., *Sakamoto Ryoma and the Meiji Restoration*, Princeton, Princeton University Press, 1961.

Craig, A., *Choshu in the Meiji Restoration*, Cambridge, Harvard University Press, 1961.

Yamamura, K., *Samurai Income and Entrepreneurship*, Cambridge, Harvard University Press, 1974.

Hall, I. P., *Mori Arinori*, Cambridge, Harvard University Press, 1973.

Pyle, K., *The New Generation in Meiji Japan*, Stanford, Stanford University Press, 1969.

Yanagida, K., *Japan's Manners and Customs in the Meiji Era* [translated by C. Terry], Tokyo, Obunsha, 1957.

Hackett, R., *Yamagata Aritomo: The Rise of Modern Japan*, Cambridge, Harvard University Press, 1971.

Rosovsky, H., 'Japan's Transition to Modern Economic Growth, 1868–1885', in H. Rosovsky (ed.), *Industrialization in Two Systems: Essays in Honor of Alexander Gerschenkron*, New York, John Wiley and Sons, 1966.

(b) OCCUPATION REFORMS

Kosaka, M., *A Hundred Million Japanese: the Postwar Experience*, Tokyo/Palo Alto, Kodansha, 1972.

Kawai, K., *Japan's American Interlude*, Chicago, University of Chicago Press, 1960.

Duke, B., *Japan's Militant Teachers*, Honolulu, University Press of Hawaii, 1973.

Reischauer, E., *The United States and Japan* (3rd. edition), Cambridge, Harvard University Press, 1965.

Henderson, D. (ed.), *The Constitution of Japan: Its First Twenty Years, 1947–67*, Seattle, University of Washington Press, 1968.

Goodman, G. K. (comp.), *The American Occupation: A Retrospective View*, Lawrence, University of Kansas, 1968.

Textor, R., *Failure in Japan*, New York, J. Day Co., 1951.

Tracy, H., *Kakemono: A Sketchbook of Japan*, London, Methuen, 1950.

Dore, R., *Land Reform in Japan*, London, Oxford University Press, 1959.

Hadley, E., *Anti-Trust in Japan*, Princeton, Princeton University Press, 1969.

Cohen, J., *Japan's Economy in War and Reconstruction*, Minneapolis, University of Minnesota Press, 1949.

CHAPTER VI

Dore, R., 'Japanese Industrialization and Developing Countries: Model, Warning or Source of Healthy Doubts?', Occasional Paper No. 8, Institute of Southeast Asian Studies, Singapore, August 1971.

Norman, E. H., *Japan's Emergence as a Modern State*, New York, Institute of Pacific Relations, 1940.

Dower, J., 'E. H. Norman, Japan and the Uses of History', in J. Dower (ed.), *Origins of the Modern Japanese State: Selected Writings of E. H. Norman*, New York, Pantheon Books, 1975.

Halliday, J., *A Political History of Japanese Capitalism*, New York, Pantheon Books, 1975.

Moore, B., *Social Origins of Dictatorship and Democracy*, Boston, Beacon Press, 1966, Chapter on Japan.

Morley, J., 'Introduction: Choice and Consequence' in

J. Morley (ed.), *Dilemmas of Growth in Prewar Japan*, Princeton, Princeton University Press, 1971.

Reischauer, E., 'What Went Wrong', in J. Morley, op. cit.

Huddell, N. and Reich, M., *Island of Dreams: Environmental Crisis in Japan*, New York, Autumn Press, 1975.

Kelly, D., *et al.*, *The Economic Superpowers and the Environment: the United States, the Soviet Union, and Japan*, San Francisco, W. H. Freeman, 1976.

Chubachi Masayoshi and Taira Koji, 'Poverty in Modern Japan', in H. Patrick (ed.), *Japanese Industrialization and its Social Consequences*, Berkeley, University of California Press, 1976.

Caldarola, C., 'The *Doya-Gai*: A Japanese Version of Skid Row', *Pacific Affairs*, Winter, 1968–9.

Index